Candlelight Cuisine
Romantic Dining

To Terry
&
Feeling Friday Forever

by
Jane Bailey

Pictured on Front Cover
Boneless Grilled Chicken with Butterflied Prawns
and Peppercorn Sauce, page 119

Candlelight Cuisine

by Jane Bailey

First Printing – January 1996

Copyright© 1996 by

Jane Bailey

Published by
Brenda Johnson
918 - 12th Street
New Westminster, British Columbia
Canada   V3M 6B1

Canadian Cataloguing in Publication Data

Bailey, Jane, 1953-

     Candlelight cuisine : romantic dining

Includes index.

ISBN 1-895292-74-3

     1. Cookery.   2. Menus.   I. Title.

TX737.B34 1996   641.5'6   C95-920813-5

Cover and page design by
Brian Danchuk
Brian Danchuk Design
Regina, Saskatchewan

Food Photography by
Ross Durant
Ross Durant Photography
Vancouver, British Columbia

Dishes and Accessories courtesy of:
Country Wreath, White Rock, B.C.
Kitchen Garden, Surrey, B.C.
Kuchenprofi
Modern Accents, Surrey, B.C.
Ocean Park Nursery, Surrey, B.C.
Pino's Interiors Ltd., White Rock, B.C.
Potager, Surrey, B.C.

Designed, Printed and Produced in Canada by
Centax Books, A Division of PrintWest Communications
Publishing Director, Photo Designer and Food Stylist – Margo Embury
1150 Eighth Avenue, Regina, Saskatchewan   Canada S4R 1C9
(306) 525-2304   Fax (306) 757-2439

Table of Contents

All recipes have been tested in U.S. Standard measurements. Common metric measurements are given as a convenience for those who are more familiar with metric. Recipes have not been tested in metric.

Introduction

Romantic dining and creating a magical ambiance for the enjoyment of superb food are Jane Bailey's special interests. As newlyweds, Jane and Terry Bailey shared weekly candlelight dinners on Friday evenings. This tradition has flourished for more than twenty years.

Jane's love of cooking led her to classes at the Cordon Bleu Cooking School in Paris and to classes with the renown Roger Verge in the south of France. Her love of good food also prompted her to start catering, an interest which evolved into a very successful gourmet take-out store and catering business, "Candlelight Cuisine and Gourmet Take-Out Foods" which she now operates with her sister, Patti Halford. A new line of specialty products includes Jane's own exotic chutneys, fruit conserves and dilled vegetables.

Jane Bailey's warmth and enthusiasm, as well as her expertise, are evident in her cooking classes and, more recently, in her television cooking demonstrations. She chooses recipes that people really respond to. Recipes that work and are wonderful for entertaining and creating a splash. Her cooking style is a skillful combination of manageability and elegance. She likes to show her students "the fun and ease of cooking well," and she adapts classic recipes "to suit the pace and realities of life today."

"Candlelight Cuisine – Romantic Dining" features outrageously good food with intriguing flavor combinations. An imaginative menu section provides stimulating ideas for romantic evenings, intimate dinner parties, alfresco dining with family and friends and, especially, candlelight tête-à-têtes with someone you love.

Appetizers

Veggie Cheese Pâté

This is a wonderfully light alternative to heavy rich pâtés. The cheesecloth creates a tiny crisscross design that is very attractive.

2 cups	pot cheese or large-curd cottage cheese	500 mL
6 oz.	radishes, trimmed and chopped	170 g
2	small red bell peppers, chopped	2
1	cucumber, peeled, seeded and chopped	1
1	bunch of watercress, rinsed well and stems removed	1
1 tbsp.	Worcestershire sauce	15 mL
1½-2 tsp.	salt, or to taste	7-10 mL
1 tsp.	dried summer savory, crumbled	5 mL
¾ tsp.	dried basil, crumbled	3 mL
¾ tsp.	dried marjoram, crumbled	3 mL
	freshly ground pepper to taste	

Method

Purée the cheese through the fine disk of a food mill into a bowl or force it through a sieve into a bowl. In a food processor or blender blend the cheese with the remaining ingredients until the mixture is smooth.

Line a 1-quart (1 L) loaf pan with a triple thickness of rinsed and squeezed cheesecloth, leaving enough overhang to fold over the top. Spoon the cheese mixture into the pan and rap sharply on the counter to expel any bubbles. Smooth the top with a spatula.

Fold the overhanging cheesecloth over the pâté and cover the top of the loaf pan with a double layer of foil. Weight the pâté with a 2-lb. (1 kg) weight and chill for at least 6 hours.

Remove the weight and foil and unfold the cheesecloth. Invert a platter over the pan and invert the pâté onto it. Discard the cheesecloth and blot any liquid. Slice the pâté and serve it with sesame melba rounds, a crusty French baguette, Herbed Focaccia, page 34, or Fresh Pita Bread, page 38.

Serves

6-10

Layered Cheese Dip

The joy of making your own nonfat cream cheese! This should become a staple in your refrigerator to substitute for cream cheese in any recipe and "lighten up"! With this flavorful topping, yogurt cheese becomes absolutely decadent.

8 oz.	nonfat cream cheese or yogurt cheese (see below)	250 g
½	red onion, diced	½
½ cup	sun-dried tomatoes, chopped	125 mL
3	large garlic cloves, minced	3
½ cup	chopped fresh basil	125 mL
1-2 tbsp.	olive oil	15-30 mL

Method Spread softened cream cheese in center of serving platter. Layer onion, tomatoes, garlic on top, ending with chopped basil. Drizzle oil over top. Surround with wedges of Herbed Focaccia, page 34. Decorate with fresh basil.

Yogurt Cheese: Line a strainer or sieve with cheesecloth or a coffee filter. Spoon into it a large container of low-fat yogurt. Cover and set over a small, deep bowl. Place in refrigerator to drain, about 8 hours.

Serves 6-10

Danish Blue Herb Bread

3 tbsp.	minced, fresh herbs (chives, basil, parsley, sage, etc.)	45 mL
1	large garlic clove, minced	1
3 tbsp.	melted butter	45 mL
1	loaf hearty, peasant bread, unsliced	1
4 tbsp.	crumbled blue cheese	60 mL
4 tbsp.	mayonnaise	60 mL
4 tbsp.	Parmesan cheese	60 mL

Combine herbs, garlic and butter and let stand 15 minutes. Preheat broiler. Split loaf lengthwise and brush with herbed butter. Broil just until golden. Meanwhile, combine blue cheese and mayonnaise and spread over bread. Top with Parmesan cheese and broil until topping is golden and bubbly.

Makes 1 loaf

Pictured on page 69.

Fiesta Loaf

The name says it all – perfect for festive occasions, easy enough for everyday! If you wish to "lighten up" simply substitute nonfat mayonnaise.

1 cup	mayonnaise	250 mL
1 cup	grated Parmesan cheese (about 3 oz. [85 g])	250 mL
1½ tsp.	minced garlic	7 mL
1 lb.	round sourdough bread, halved horizontally	500 g
	butter	
3 tbsp.	finely chopped fresh basil or 2 tsp. (10 mL) dried, crumbled basil	45 mL

Preheat broiler. Mix mayonnaise, Parmesan and garlic in large bowl to blend. Arrange bread, cut side up, on large baking sheet. Butter bread. Broil until crisp and brown. Spread Parmesan mixture over cut sides of bread. Broil until top is puffed and golden brown. Sprinkle with chopped basil. Cut into wedges and serve.

Makes   12 servings

Barbecued Pesto French Bread

1	baguette (long French loaf)	1
1 cup	chopped fresh parsley	250 mL
2 tbsp.	dried basil or 6 tbsp. (90 mL) fresh basil	30 mL
½ cup	Parmesan cheese	125 mL
½ cup	pine nuts	125 mL
2	large garlic cloves	2
⅓ cup	olive oil	75 mL
	Parmesan cheese	
	pimiento	

Slice baguette lengthwise; process next 5 ingredients. With motor running, slowly pour in olive oil to make a thick paste. Spread on bread; sprinkle with more cheese and with pimiento. Wrap in foil and grill until heated through, about 10-15 minutes.

Makes   1 loaf

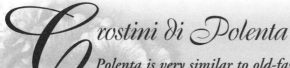

Crostini di Polenta

Polenta is very similar to old-fashioned Cream of Wheat.
The texture and the topping provide an unusual taste sensation.

Polenta Toast:

¼ cup	finely chopped onion	60 mL
1 tbsp.	extra light olive oil	15 mL
1½ cups	chicken broth	375 mL
1 cup	water	250 mL
⅔ cup	yellow cornmeal	150 mL
1 tbsp.	grated Parmesan cheese	15 mL
	salt to taste	

Roasted Peppers with Herbs:

7 oz.	jar roasted red peppers, rinsed and drained	200 g
1 tbsp.	extra light olive oil	15 mL
1 tbsp.	chopped fresh basil or parsley	15 mL
	salt to taste	

Method

Polenta Toast: Combine onion and olive oil in a 4-quart (4 L) saucepan, stirring over low heat until tender, about 5 minutes. Stir in broth. In a separate bowl combine water and cornmeal; stir into the broth and cook, stirring, until the mixture boils and is thick, about 10 minutes. Add cheese and salt to taste.

Line a 9" (23 cm) square baking pan with foil; spray foil lightly with olive oil cooking spray. Spread polenta (cornmeal mixture) in a smooth layer with spatula. Refrigerate until cold and firm, about 2 hours. Turn polenta out of pan and peel off foil. Cut polenta into triangles. Preheat oven to 425°F (220°C). Spray a nonstick baking sheet with olive oil cooking spray. Arrange triangles on pan so they do not touch each other.

Bake on bottom rack until browned on bottom, about 15 minutes. Turn and bake until browned and crisp.

Meanwhile, cut peppers into even portions. Drizzle with olive oil and sprinkle with herbs and salt. Arrange on top of each baked triangle.

Serve warm or at room temperature.

Serves   8

Pesto Prawn Pizzas with Artichokes

Pizza Bases:

1 cup	white plain flour	250 mL
½ cup	whole-wheat flour	125 mL
1 tbsp.	yeast (7 g env.)	15 mL
1 tsp.	sugar	5 mL
¼ cup	warm water	60 mL
¼ cup	warm milk	60 mL
2 tbsp.	olive oil	30 mL

Pesto:

2 tbsp.	pine nuts, toasted	30 mL
1 cup	firmly packed basil leaves	250 mL
1	garlic clove, crushed	1
2 tbsp.	grated fresh Parmesan cheese	30 mL
⅓ cup	olive oil	75 mL
12	cooked prawns, shelled	12
12	bottled drained artichoke hearts, halved	12
1 cup	grated mozzarella cheese	250 mL

Method

Pizza Bases: Sift flours into large bowl. Dissolve yeast and sugar in warm water add milk and oil; add flour and mix to a firm dough. Turn dough onto floured surface; knead for about 5 minutes, or until dough is smooth and elastic. Return dough to greased bowl, cover, stand in warm place about 1 hour, or until dough is doubled in size.

Turn dough onto lightly floured surface, knead until smooth. Divide into 6 portions, roll each portion to a 4" (10 cm) round. Place rounds on lightly greased oven trays; shape sides to form pizza cases.

Pesto: Blend or process all ingredients until smooth.

Spread pesto evenly over pizza bases; top with prawns and artichokes; sprinkle with cheese. Bake in 375°F (190°C) oven about 15 minutes, or until pizzas are browned.

Makes 6 mini pizzas

Wine-Soaked Camembert and Toasted Almonds

This very romantic appetizer is perfect for two, when using the 4½ oz. (130 g) round of Camembert. For a larger group a bigger round of Camembert encased in golden almonds is a visual delight.

4½ oz.	Camembert	130 g
¾ cup	dry white wine	175 mL
4 oz.	butter, softened	125 g
	few drops Tabasco	
3 oz.	flaked almonds	90 g

Method

Place Camembert in small bowl and cover with the wine; cover and leave overnight. Next day, drain off the wine, chop Camembert roughly, including the rind. Put into small bowl of electric mixer. Add softened butter and a few drops of Tabasco; beat on medium speed until the mixture is smooth and well blended. Refrigerate 5 minutes.

Place flaked almonds on an oven tray; bake in moderate oven 5 minutes, or until pale golden brown; cool.

Shape cheese mixture into original shape of cheese. Roll top and sides of cheese in toasted almonds, patting them on firmly with hands. Refrigerate until firm. Remove from refrigerator 30 minutes before serving. Serve with garlic or sesame Melba rounds.

Serves 2

Mediterranean Baked Brie

What a wonderful do-ahead appetizer! Put it together well ahead and simply bake at the last moment. Garnish with fresh sprigs of rosemary.

8 oz.	wheel or wedge of Brie	250 g
6 oz.	jar marinated artichoke hearts, drained and coarsely chopped	184 mL
1-2	red bell peppers, halved, seeded, roasted, peeled and coarsely chopped	1-2
	minced fresh rosemary to taste	
½ cup	garlic cloves, roasted (see page 84)	125 mL

Method

Preheat the oven to 350°F (180°C). Place the Brie in an attractive oven-proof dish. Mix together the remaining ingredients and pour over the Brie. Place in the oven and bake until the cheese just begins to melt, 10-15 minutes. Serve with French bread or assorted crackers.

Serves 4-6

Pictured on the back cover.

Brie en Brioche

What a beautiful centerpiece! Surround this beauty with giant strawberries and purple grapes – at Christmas try a huge plaid bow!

Brioche Dough:

1 tbsp.	yeast (7 g env.)	15 mL
¼ cup	warm water	60 mL
2 tbsp.	flour	30 mL
¼ cup	butter	60 mL
1 tbsp.	sugar	15 mL
⅓ cup	milk	75 mL
½ tsp.	salt	5 mL
7	eggs, at room temperature	7
4-5 cups	flour	1-1.25 L
¾ cup	butter	175 mL
1 lb.	Brie	500 g
1	egg yolk	1
1 tbsp.	water	15 mL

Method

Dissolve yeast in warm water, then add 2 tbsp. (30 mL) flour to make a sponge. Set aside. Warm butter, sugar, milk and salt. Beat eggs until smooth; add warmed milk mixture and yeast sponge. Mix in enough flour to make a soft dough. Knead for a few minutes then put in a clean bowl and smear the ¾ cup (175 mL) butter over the top. Cover and let rise in a warm place until doubled. Punch dough down and slap around until it loses its stringiness and butter is worked in. Refrigerate until cool.

Roll out dough and place the round of Brie in the center. Wrap well and seal seams. Brush with egg yolk beaten with water.

Bake at 375°F (190°C) about 45 minutes. Let bread rest a while so cheese won't be too runny, about 15-20 minutes.

Serves

10-15

Pictured on page 17.

Herbed Tomato Brioche and Smoked Salmon-Cream Cheese Brioche

Prepare brioche dough as on previous page.

Divide dough into 2 parts, one for each filling. (Recipes for fillings to follow.)

Roll each half out. Cut in half again. Fit 1 piece into a buttered bundt pan or brioche pan. Spoon filling into pan. Top with another piece of dough; crimp edges. Brush with a beaten egg. Bake at 375°F (190°C) about 30-40 minutes.

Fillings

Herbed Tomato Filling:

4	large tomatoes, peeled and cored	4
4 tbsp.	butter	60 mL
1 tbsp.	minced fresh basil	15 mL
1 tbsp.	minced fresh oregano	15 mL
	salt and pepper	
8 oz.	mozzarella cheese, diced	250 g
½ cup	Parmesan cheese	125 mL

Method In a 350°F (180°C) oven, bake tomatoes in a buttered dish for 15 minutes. Drain off juices and seeds. Dot each tomato with 1 tbsp. (15 mL) butter. Bake 1½ hours. Using a fork, mash tomatoes. Stir in basil, oregano, salt and pepper. Cool. Stir in cheeses.

Smoked Salmon Filling:

8 oz.	cream cheese, softened	250 g
¼ lb.	smoked salmon	125 g
1 tbsp.	minced dillweed	15 mL

Method Whip all of the ingredients together.

Quesadillas with Brie, Mango and Chilies

This is such a fun appetizer for summer grilling. The flavors are incredible.

1	poblano chili	1
1	red bell pepper	1
½ cup	water	125 mL
1	medium onion, thinly sliced	1
2 tbsp.	butter, melted	30 mL
2 tbsp.	vegetable oil	30 mL
1	ripe mango, peeled, pitted, chopped	1
2 tbsp.	chopped fresh cilantro	30 mL
8 oz.	chilled Brie cheese, rind trimmed cut into ¼" (1 cm) wide strips	250 g
4	8" (20 cm) flour tortillas	4

Method Char chili and bell pepper over gas flame or under broiler until blackened on all sides. Wrap in paper bag and let stand 10 minutes to steam. Peel, core and seed. Rinse if necessary; pat dry and chop. Place in small bowl.

Bring ½ cup (125 mL) water to boil in heavy saucepan. Add onion. Cover and remove from heat. Let stand until onion is wilted, about 10 minutes. Drain. Add onion to chili mixture.

Heat barbecue to medium or preheat broiler. Blend melted butter and vegetable oil in small bowl. Add chopped mango and chopped fresh cilantro to chili mixture. Place ¼ of Brie cheese strips on half of each flour tortilla. Top each with ¼ of chili-mango mixture. Season with salt and pepper. Fold over empty half of flour tortillas to enclose filling. Brush with butter mixture. Place quesadillas, buttered side down, on grill. Cook 30 seconds, turn quesadillas 90 degrees and grill 30 seconds. Butter uncooked side and turn over. Grill until cheese begins to melt, about 30 seconds. Cut each quesadilla into 3 pieces. Arrange quesadillas on platter and serve.

Serves 4

Jalapeño Cheese Squares

Great do-ahead fare. Make it as hot or as cool as your taste buds allow by increasing or decreasing chilies.

10	large eggs	10
¼ cup	minced fresh jalapeño chilies	60 mL
2 tbsp.	chili powder	30 mL
4 tsp.	ground cumin	20 mL
1½ cups	whole milk (not low fat)	375 mL
4 cups	grated Monterey Jack cheese (about 1 lb. [500 g])	1 L
2 cups	chopped green onions (about 12)	500 mL
4 cups	grated Cheddar cheese (about 1 lb. [500 g])	1 L

Method Preheat oven to 350°F (180°C). Butter 2, 9" (23 cm) square glass baking dishes. Whisk first 4 ingredients in large bowl to blend. Whisk in milk. Add Monterey Jack cheese and onions and stir to combine. Divide mixture between prepared dishes. Sprinkle half of Cheddar cheese over each dish

Bake until tops are light brown and puffed, about 45 minutes. Cool slightly. Cut into 1½" (1.3 cm) squares. This can be prepared 8 hours ahead.

Transfer squares to large heavy cookie sheet. Cover and refrigerate. Before serving, rewarm in 350°F (180°C) oven until heated through, about 10 minutes. Transfer cheese squares to platter and serve.

Makes about 72 squares

Bacon-Wrapped Chutney Bananas

2	bananas, peeled	2
	fresh lemon juice	
8-10	bacon slices (uncooked), halved crosswise	8-10
1 cup	mango chutney	250 mL

Method Preheat oven to 375°F (190°C). Cut bananas into crosswise slices the same width as bacon strips. Roll in lemon juice. Wrap each banana piece in half bacon strip; secure with toothpick. Arrange on baking sheet. Bake until bacon is almost cooked, about 20 minutes. Meanwhile, place chutney in processor and mince finely using about 5 on/off turns, or mince by hand. Dip bacon-wrapped banana pieces into chutney to coat evenly. Return to baking sheet and continue baking until crisp, 5-10 minutes.

Serves 6

Curried Sweet Tater Skins

This is a colorful alternative to regular potato skins. Serve with sour cream and applesauce for dipping.

3	large sweet potatoes (about 1½ lbs. [750 g])	3
2 tbsp.	butter or margarine, melted	30 mL
1 cup	shredded Monterey Jack Cheese with jalapeño peppers (4 oz. [125 g])	250 mL
¼ cup	finely chopped peanuts	60 mL
1 tsp.	curry powder	5 mL
⅛ tsp.	ground cumin	0.5 mL

Method Scrub potatoes and prick with a fork. Bake at 425°F (220°C) for 40-50 minutes, or until tender. Halve crosswise and lengthwise. (If pieces are too large, cut lengthwise again.) Scoop out insides leaving ¼" (1 cm) shells; save pulp for another use. Brush both sides of skin with melted butter. Place skins on baking dish cut-side up. Bake at 425°F (220°C) for 10-12 minutes, or until crisp.

Combine cheese, peanuts, curry powder and cumin in a bowl. Toss to mix well. Spoon cheese mixture onto potato skins; return to oven for 2-3 minutes more, or until cheese is melted. Serve warm.

Makes about 18

Appetizer

Brie en Brioche, page 12

Pesto-Stuffed Mushrooms

A low-fat, high-flavor appetizer.

16	large mushrooms	16
3 tbsp.	minced onions	45 mL
2 tsp.	minced garlic	10 mL
2 tsp.	olive oil	10 mL
2 tbsp.	fine rye bread crumbs	30 mL
⅓ cup	minced fresh basil	75 mL
2 tbsp.	minced fresh parsley	30 mL
1 tsp.	dried oregano	5 mL
	black pepper	
	pinch of salt	
	shredded soya "mozzarella"	

Method Remove stems from mushrooms; mince the stems. Place caps, round side up, on baking sheet and broil 3-5 minutes. Sauté onion and garlic in oil for 5 minutes, stirring often. Add the minced stems and crumbs. Cook 3 minutes. Remove from heat; add remaining ingredients except cheese. Arrange caps in sprayed baking pan, hollow side up. Fill with basil-crumb mixture. Sprinkle with cheese. Broil 3-5 minutes.

Makes 16

Pictured on the back cover.

Wild Mushroom Phyllo Filling

What a joy phyllo pastry is! Good phyllo should not be torn or shredded. Fresh is the very best but it is not always available. Inquire at Greek restaurants to see if you can purchase phyllo pastry from them.

1 tbsp.	butter	15 mL
1 tbsp.	olive oil	15 mL
1½ lbs.	chanterelle or shiitake mushrooms, coarsely chopped	750 g
½ cup	nonfat sour cream	125 mL
¾ cup	chopped parsley	175 mL
	salt and pepper to taste	
	freshly ground nutmeg to taste	

Method In a skillet, melt the butter with the oil over high heat; add mushrooms and sauté 2-3 minutes. Remove from heat and cool slightly. Add the sour cream and chopped parsley to the mushrooms. Season to taste with salt, pepper and nutmeg. Cool completely before filling phyllo. Use phyllo amounts and directions as on page 20 or 21.

Serves 6

Phyllo Spring Rolls with Sun-Dried Tomato Aioli

1	small carrot	1
⅔ cup	fresh green beans	150 mL
1	small zucchini	1
1	small green pepper	1
½ tsp.	finely shredded lemon peel	2 mL
1	large garlic clove, crushed	1
6	sheets frozen phyllo dough (18 x 14" [45 x 35 cm]), thawed	6
6 tbsp.	melted butter or margarine	90 mL
	Cajun spice	

Method Cut vegetables into thin 2" (5 cm) strips. Cook carrots and green beans, covered, in boiling salted water for 5 minutes. Drain well. Toss all vegetables in bowl with lemon peel and garlic.

Phyllo Assembly: Lightly brush 1 sheet of phyllo dough with some melted butter. Place another sheet of phyllo on top of first sheet and brush with melted butter. Repeat with another sheet of phyllo and butter. Cut into 12 squares about 4 x 4" (10 x 10 cm). Place about 8 vegetables strips in center of a square. Fold in both sides. Fold bottom edge over vegetables and roll up. Repeat with remaining dough, butter and vegetables. Place on ungreased baking sheet. Brush tops with remaining butter; sprinkle with Cajun spice. Bake at 375°F (190°C) until golden, 15-18 minutes.

Meanwhile, prepare the Sun-Dried Tomato Aioli (below).

Serves 6

Pictured on the back cover.

Sun-Dried Tomato Aioli

½ cup	sun-dried tomatoes	125 mL
1 cup	mayonnaise	250 mL
¼ cup	lemon juice	60 mL
4	garlic cloves, minced	4
1 tbsp.	Dijon-style mustard	15 mL

Method Pour boiling water over dried tomatoes; let stand 30 minutes and drain. Chop tomatoes coarsely and process in food processor until puréed. Add mayonnaise, lemon juice, garlic and mustard to processor. Process with a few on/off turns. Serve with the warm spring rolls.

Makes 1½ cups (375 mL)

Sun-Dried Tomato and Scallop Phyllos

Any of these phyllo recipes can be prepared completely ahead and frozen prior to baking.

Sun-Dried Tomato and Scallop Filling:

½ cup	sun-dried tomatoes	125 mL
2	large garlic cloves	2
2 tbsp.	chopped fresh parsley	30 mL
2 tbsp.	chopped fresh basil	30 mL
1 tsp.	cayenne pepper	5 mL
1	green onion, chopped	1
¼ cup	pine nuts	60 mL
4 oz.	nonfat or light cream cheese	125 g
12	scallops	12
¼ cup	chicken stock	60 mL

Phyllo Triangles:

3	phyllo sheets	3
	melted butter	

Method

Filling: Chop first 7 ingredients in processor. Add cream cheese; process on and off. Meanwhile, sauté scallops in chicken stock about 2 minutes. Place 1 tbsp. (15 mL) tomato mixture and a scallop on each triangle. Roll as directed.

Phyllo Assembly: For phyllo triangles, melt and cool the butter. Place 1 sheet of phyllo on a flat surface and brush lightly with the butter. Top this with 2 more sheets, buttering each. Cut the sheets in half lengthwise, then cut each half crosswise into 6 equal parts. Spoon a teaspoon (5 mL) of filling onto the end of each strip and form a triangle by folding the right-hand corner to the opposite side, as you would a flag. Continue folding until entire strip is used.

Preheat oven to 400°F (200°C). Place triangles on a buttered baking sheet. Brush the tops of each with melted butter and bake until golden brown, about 10 minutes.

Makes 12 phyllo triangles

Phyllo Triangles with Sausage and Mustard

This unique phyllo pastry puts the classic sausage roll to shame!

Sausage and Mustard Filling:

1 lb.	sweet Italian sausage, removed from casing and crumbled	500 g
1 cup	whipping cream	250 mL
¼ cup	Dijon mustard	60 mL
½ tsp.	freshly grated nutmeg	2 mL
10	phyllo sheets	10
1 cup	unsalted butter	250 mL

Method

Filling: Cook sausage in heavy, medium-sized skillet over medium heat until no longer pink and fat is rendered, stirring frequently with fork, about 15 minutes. Strain through fine sieve, pressing to extract as much moisture as possible. Drain on paper towels. Wipe out skillet. Return sausage to skillet. Stir in cream, mustard and nutmeg. Stirring frequently, simmer until sausage absorbs cream and mixture mounds on spoon, about 15 minutes. Cool.

Phyllo Assembly: Butter 2 baking sheets. Place 1 phyllo sheet on work surface. Keep remainder covered with a damp towel to prevent drying. Brush with melted butter. Place another sheet over first and brush with butter. Cut crosswise into 5 strips. Place heaping teaspoon (10 mL) of sausage mixture at bottom of 1 strip. Fold a corner of phyllo over sausage, to the other side, creating a triangle, and brush lightly with butter. Continue folding down entire length of strip, brushing lightly with butter after each fold. Repeat with remaining strips. Arrange on prepared sheets, spacing 1" (2.5 cm) apart. Brush with butter. Repeat with remaining phyllo and filling. This can be prepared one day ahead and refrigerated.

Preheat oven to 350°F (180°C). Bake pastries until golden brown and crisp, 20-25 minutes. Drain on paper towels. Serve phyllo triangles hot or warm.

Freezing

These can also be prepared 1 month ahead. Freeze on unbuttered sheets until firm. Wrap tightly and return to freezer. To bake, arrange unthawed triangles on buttered sheets. Bake in 325°F (160°C) oven until golden brown and crisp, 40-45 minutes.

Makes

25 phyllo triangles

Cajun Pork Phyllos with Apricot Dip

Cajun Pork Filling:

16 oz.	ground pork	250 g
2 tsp.	Cajun seasoning	10 mL
1 cup	soft-style cream cheese	250 mL
⅔ cup	shredded carrot	150 mL
	few dashes of hot pepper sauce	
12	sheets frozen phyllo dough thawed	12
	(18 x 14" [45 x 35 cm] sheets)	
½ cup	butter or margarine, melted	125 mL
	additional melted butter or margarine	
	Apricot Dipping Sauce	
	(optional), (below)	

Method

Filling: In a medium skillet, cook pork until no longer pink; drain. Add Cajun seasoning and cook 1 minute. Stir in cream cheese, carrot and hot sauce. Mix well. Makes about 2 cups (500 mL) of filling.

Phyllo Assembly: Lightly brush 1 sheet of phyllo dough with some of the melted butter or margarine. Place another sheet of phyllo dough on top of the first sheet, then brush with butter or margarine. Cover remaining phyllo with a damp cloth to keep moist; set aside.

Cut the 2 layered sheets crosswise into 6 equal strips. To make each triangle, spoon 1 rounded teaspoon (10 mL) of Cajun Pork Filling about 1" (2.5 cm) from 1 end of 1 of the strips. Starting at the same end of the phyllo strip, fold 1 of the points over the filling so it lines up with the other side of the strip, forming a triangle. Continue folding like a flag in a triangular shape, using the entire strip of phyllo dough. Repeat 5 more times with the remaining sheets of phyllo dough, butter and filling.

Makes

3 dozen phyllo triangles

Apricot Dipping Sauce

3 tbsp.	apricot preserves, melted	45 mL
½ cup	plain yogurt or sour cream	125 mL
1 tbsp.	balsamic vinegar	15 mL

Method

Whisk all ingredients together.

Éclairs au Jambon

Remember old-fashioned cream puffs? Well, this French starter uses that classic pastry to encase a succulent cheese and ham filling.

Pâte à Choux:

½ cup	butter, cut into pieces	125 mL
pinch	salt	pinch
pinch	grated nutmeg	pinch
pinch	sugar	pinch
1 cup	water	250 mL
1 cup + 2 tbsp.	all-purpose flour	275 mL
4	eggs, at room temperature, beaten	4

Cheese and Ham Filling:

¼ cup	butter	60 mL
¾ cup	flour	175 mL
2¼ cups	milk	550 mL
1 cup	finely grated Gruyère or Cheddar cheese	250 mL
½ cup	chopped mushrooms, sautéed in butter	125 mL
½ cup	chopped processed ham	125 mL
	a little chopped truffle	
	salt, pepper, nutmeg to taste	

Toppings:

12	thin slices processed ham	12
1 cup	grated Gruyère or Cheddar cheese	250 mL
6	thin slices of bacon, cooked, crumbled	6
	strips of tomato to garnish	

Method

Pâte à Choux: Place the butter, salt, nutmeg, sugar and water in a saucepan over low heat. When the butter has melted, bring to a boil and add all the flour at once. Beat vigorously until the mixture forms a ball which leaves the sides of the pan clean. Cool slightly, then beat in the eggs, one at a time, until thoroughly mixed. Do not replace pan on the heat.

Place the mixture in a piping bag, fitted with a ¾" (2 cm) plain nozzle. Pipe 12 lines of dough, about 4" (10 cm) long, onto greased baking sheets, spacing them well apart. Cook in preheated 425°F (200°C) oven for about 30 minutes, or until éclairs are well-puffed, browned and firm to the touch. Make a slit along the side of each one to release the steam and return to the oven for 5 minutes, or until crisp. Cut in half, cool on a wire rack and remove any remaining soft dough from the centers of the éclairs.

Éclairs au Jambon

Continued

Filling: Melt butter in a saucepan over low heat. Beat in flour and cook for 1-2 minutes. Stir in milk gradually; bring to a boil, stirring constantly. Cook until sauce is thick and smooth. Add cheese, mushrooms, ham and truffle. Season to taste with salt, pepper and nutmeg. Allow to cool.

When cold, fill the éclairs with two-thirds of the sauce and wrap each in a slice of ham. Coat with some of the remaining sauce and roll in the grated cheese. Top with crumbled bacon and tomato. Brown on top rack of a 475°F (240°C) oven immediately before serving.

Makes 12 eclairs

Spicy Stuffed Crab

2	large whole cooked crabs	2
2 cups	fresh white bread crumbs	500 mL
½ cup	milk	125 mL
2 tbsp.	vegetable oil	30 mL
1 cup	chopped onion	250 mL
2	large garlic cloves, chopped	2
2 tbsp.	chopped fresh chives	30 mL
2 tsp.	chopped jalapeño peppers	10 mL
1 tsp.	thyme	5 mL
¼ tsp.	ground cloves	1 mL
3 tbsp.	lemon juice	45 mL
2 tbsp.	lime juice	30 mL
½ cup	sour cream	125 mL
	salt and pepper to taste	
	lime zest	

Method Preheat oven to 350°F (180°C). Remove crab meat from shells; reserve body shells. Place crumbs in bowl. Add milk and crab meat and mix well.

Heat oil in heavy pan over medium heat. Add onion, garlic, chives, jalapeño, thyme and cloves and sauté until onion is tender, about 4 minutes. Add crab meat mixture. Cook 2 minutes, stirring constantly. Mix in juices and sour cream. Remove from heat and season with salt and pepper.

Spoon crab mixture into reserved shells. Sprinkle with zest. Bake until heated through, about 10 minutes. Serve as a first course on 2 small plates or as a platter presentation.

Hot Tip! To extend the crab meat in this recipe, add 4 oz. (113 g) tin of crab meat, 1 cup (250 mL) crab flakes or crab or lobster substitute.

Serves 2

Pictured on the back cover.

Scallop Bundles

12	large scallops	12
1 tbsp.	butter	15 mL
1	garlic clove	1
3 oz.	pkg. smoked salmon cream cheese	85 g
¼ cup	finely chopped purple onion	60 mL
2 tbsp.	chopped red pepper	30mL
½ tsp.	Worcestershire sauce	2 mL
	few dashes of Tabasco sauce	
8 oz.	frozen puff pastry	250 g
1	egg, beaten	1

Method   Sauté scallops in butter with a garlic clove for 5 minutes. Combine with next 5 ingredients in a mixing bowl. Set aside. Roll out puff pastry to large square, cut into 12, 4" (10 cm) squares. Place a rounded tablespoon of filling on each square. Top with 1 scallop. Bring the 4 corners of the pastry together and twist. Brush with beaten egg. Arrange on foil-lined baking sheet. Bake 12-15 minutes at 400°F (200°C). Serve with warm jalapeño jelly.

Makes   12 appetizers

Spinach Sausage Squares

3 tbsp.	vegetable oil	45 mL
1	onion, chopped	1
1 lb.	sweet Italian sausages, removed from casings and crumbled	500 g
2 x 10 oz.	pkgs. frozen spinach, defrosted, squeezed dry and chopped	2 x 283 g
1 cup	soda cracker crumbs	250 mL
4	eggs	4
½ cup	milk or cream	125 mL
	salt and pepper to taste	
1 cup	grated Cheddar cheese	250 mL

Method   Heat oil in large skillet. Cook onion until lightly browned. Add sausage and break up well with spoon. Cook 10 minutes, until browned. Drain off excess fat and discard. Stir in spinach and cook a few minutes. Cool slightly. Stir in cracker crumbs. Beat eggs with milk, salt, pepper and cheese. Stir in sausage-spinach mixture. Spoon into a buttered 9" (23 cm) square baking dish. Bake in preheated 350°F (180°C) oven for 35-40 minutes, or until set in the center. This can be made ahead and served cold or at room temperature, cut into squares, or it can be reheated at 350°F (180°C) for 20 minutes. Allow to rest 10 minutes before cutting.

Serves   6-8

Mahogany Chicken Wings

1½ cups	soy sauce	375 mL
¾ cup	dry sherry*	175 mL
1⅛ cups	hoisin sauce*	280 mL
¾ cup	Chinese plum sauce	175 mL
18	green onions, minced	18
6	garlic cloves, minced	6
¾ cup	cider vinegar	175 mL
½ cup	honey	125 mL
6-7 lbs.	chicken wings	2.5-3 kg

Method In 3-quart (3 L) saucepan, combine all ingredients except wings. Bring to a boil and simmer 5 minutes. Cool.

While sauce is cooling, cut off wing tips and set aside for stockpot. Separate wings at joints and place in large storage container. Pour cooled sauce over, cover and refrigerate overnight.

Place oven racks in upper and lower thirds of oven and preheat to 375°F (190°C). Oil 2 large shallow roasting pans.

Drain wings. Divide between prepared pans and bake, uncovered, 1-1½ hours. Baste about every 20 minutes with remaining sauce and turn ribs to brown. Be sure to switch the pans halfway through cooking.

Remove wings from pans and let cool on large sheets of foil. When cool, wrap and store for up to 3 days. Serve at room temperature.

Serves 20

*Both of these products are available in Oriental food stores or gourmet shops.

Pictured on the back cover.

Crunchy Western Wings with Parsley Cream

3 lbs.	chicken wings	2 kg
1 cup	all-purpose flour	250 mL
1 cup	cornmeal	250 mL
2 tbsp.	ground cumin	30 mL
2 tsp.	pepper flakes	10 mL
2 tsp.	salt	10 mL
2 tsp.	black pepper	10 mL
1 tsp.	cayenne pepper	5 mL
3	eggs	3
¼ cup	olive or vegetable oil	60 mL

Method　Remove tips from chicken wings; separate wings at joints. Set aside.

In shallow dish, combine flour, cornmeal, cumin, pepper flakes, salt and black and cayenne peppers.

In another shallow dish, beat eggs. Dip wings into flour mixture shaking off excess; dip into eggs, allowing excess to drain off. Dip again into flour mixture and press mixture in firmly.

Brush baking sheets with oil; arrange wings on sheets and drizzle with remaining oil. Bake in 375°F (190°C) oven for 20 minutes; turn wings over and bake for 20-25 minutes longer, or until brown, crisp and no longer pink inside. Serve wings with Parsley Cream (below) on large platter.

Makes　30 wings

Parsley Cream

2 cups	sour cream (low-fat if preferred)	500 mL
1 cup	chopped fresh parsley	250 mL
¼ cup	chopped fresh coriander	60 mL
¼ cup	chopped shallots	60 mL
¼ cup	chopped green onion	60 mL
1 tbsp.	capers	15 mL
1	jalapeño pepper, seeded and minced	1
1 tsp.	salt	5 mL
	fresh pepper to taste	

Method　In bowl, whisk all ingredients together.

Makes　about 2½ cups (625 mL) of dip

Breads

Sage Biscuits and Pumpkin Butter

1¾ cups	all-purpose flour	425 mL
1 tbsp.	sugar	15 mL
1 tbsp.	fresh thyme or 1 tsp. (5 mL) dried	15 mL
1 tbsp.	fresh sage or 1 tsp. (5 mL) dried	5 mL
1 tsp.	salt	5 mL
1 tbsp.	baking powder	15 mL
6 tbsp.	chilled butter	90 mL
¾ cup	cold whipping cream	175 mL
1	egg, beaten	1
	thyme and sage	

Method Process dry ingredients and herbs until blended. Using on and off, process chilled butter with dry mixture. Slowly add cold cream and process only until blended. Turn dough onto floured surface and knead until soft and pliable. Roll out dough about ½" (1.3 cm) thick and cut into rounds. Place on an ungreased baking sheet about 1" (2.5 cm) apart. Brush with beaten egg and sprinkle with additional thyme and sage. Bake at 450°F (230°C) about 10 minutes. Serve with Pumpkin Butter (below).

Makes 6-8 biscuits

Pumpkin Butter

1	small lemon	1
14 oz.	can pumpkin	398 mL
½ cup	apple juice	125 mL
½ cup	brown sugar	125 mL
½ tsp.	salt	2 mL
½ tsp.	ginger	2 mL
½ tsp.	cinnamon	2 mL
½ tsp.	allspice	2 mL

Method Grate lemon peel and squeeze enough juice to make 1 tbsp. (15 mL). In a small saucepan, heat peel, juice and remaining ingredients to boiling. Reduce heat to low, cook ½ hour longer, stirring often. Cover and chill at least 3 hours. Serve with biscuits.

Makes 1¾ cups (425 mL)

Glazed Pecan Biscuits

Honey Orange Glaze:

2 tbsp.	honey	30 mL
3 tbsp.	frozen orange juice concentrate, thawed	45 mL

Pecan Biscuits:

3 cups	unbleached all-purpose flour	750 mL
3½ tsp.	baking powder	17 mL
2 tsp.	grated orange peel	10 mL
¾ tsp.	baking soda	3 mL
¾ tsp.	salt	3 mL
¼ tsp.	ground ginger	1 mL
¾ cup	chilled unsalted butter (1½ sticks), cut into ½" (1.3 cm) pieces	175 mL
¾ cup	finely chopped pecans (about 3 oz. [85 g])	175 mL
1 cup	plain nonfat yogurt	250 mL
3 tbsp.	honey	45 mL
	halved pecans for garnish	

Glaze: Mix honey and orange juice in a small heavy saucepan; bring to boil. Reduce heat; simmer until slightly thickened, about 3 minutes. Set aside.

Biscuits: Position rack in center of oven and preheat to 425°F (220°C). Combine flour, baking powder, orange peel, baking soda, salt and ginger in a bowl. Add butter and rub in with fingertips or mix in a food processor, processing on and off. Add pecans, yogurt and honey, mixing just until blended. Knead slightly on a floured surface. Form dough into a long roll and slice about 1" (2.5 cm) thick. Place on a greased cookie sheet and brush with glaze. Top each biscuit with a pecan half, if desired. Bake about 12-15 minutes, until golden. Brush again with glaze.

Makes   14-16 biscuits

Cin-Apple Buns

I created this wonderful recipe for my health-happy Dad. Positively fat free! Positively fantastic!! Eat with a clear conscience!!!

3 cups	flour (approx.)	750 mL
2 tbsp.	instant yeast	30 mL
2 tbsp.	sugar	30 mL
1½ tsp.	salt	10 mL
½ cup	egg whites	125 mL
1 cup	warm water (approx.)	250 mL
1½ cups	unsweetened applesauce	375 mL
2 cups	raisins	500 mL
2 tbsp.	cinnamon	30 mL
1 cup	brown sugar	250 mL
2	large tart apples	2
2 tbsp.	water	30 mL
2 tbsp.	brown sugar	30 mL

Vanilla Icing:

¼ cup	icing sugar	60 mL
1 tsp.	vanilla	5 mL
1 tsp.	hot water	5 mL

Method

In food processor, combine flour, yeast, sugar and salt. With machine running, add egg whites and water. If dough is too dry, add more water; if too wet, add more flour. Process until smooth ball forms, about 4 minutes. Cover dough with damp towel and leave on floured surface to rise – about ½ hour.

When dough has risen, roll into large rectangle. Spread applesauce over dough, then top with 1 cup (250 mL) brown sugar, raisins and cinnamon.

Meanwhile, slice unpeeled apples thinly and simmer in 2 tbsp. (30 mL) water and 2 tbsp. (30 mL) brown sugar for 4 minutes. Spread over dough and roll up as a jelly roll. Slice into 9 thick slices (12 if smaller buns desired). Spray 9 x 12" (23 x 30 cm) cake pan with nonstick spray. Place slices in cake pan. Cover and let rise about 1 hour. Bake at 375°F (190°C) for about 30 minutes.

Icing: Combine all ingredients. Icing should be very thin. After baking buns, drizzle with icing.

Yield

9-12 buns

Basil Nectarine Flatbread

There's nothing "store-bought" about this grilled flatbread!

1	loaf frozen bread dough (thawed)	1
2 tbsp.	olive oil	30 mL
2	nectarines, thinly sliced	2
1 tbsp.	balsamic or rice vinegar	15 mL
1 cup	shredded Jack cheese	250 mL
½ cup	Parmesan cheese	125 mL
2 tbsp.	chopped fresh basil	30 mL
	pine nuts	

Method   Cut loaf into 4 pieces. Roll each piece into a 6" (15 cm) round. Brush with olive oil and let rise about ½ hour. Heat the barbecue.

Transfer rounds carefully, oiled side down, to barbecue. Grill one side only, 3-4 minutes, until browned. Transfer to cookie sheet, browned side up and proceed as follows.

Mix nectarines with vinegar.

Top each bread round with both cheeses. Scatter nectarines over each round. Sprinkle with basil and pine nuts.

Return to grill; close lid and cook until toppings melt and bottom is brown.

Makes   4 flatbreads

Herbed Focaccia

5 cups	flour (approx.)	1.25 L
2 tbsp.	instant yeast (2, 7 g env.)	30 mL
2 tbsp.	sugar	30 mL
2 tsp.	salt	10 mL
1 tbsp.	chopped fresh basil	15 mL
1 tbsp.	chopped fresh thyme	15 mL
1 tsp.	dry oregano	5 mL
1 tbsp.	coarse pepper	15 mL
2⅔ cups	warm water (approx.)	650 mL
3 tbsp.	olive oil	45 mL

Method

In dough mixer or food processor, mix together all the dry ingredients and the herbs. Slowly add the water and oil. If too wet, add more flour; if too dry, add more water. Keep mixing or processing until a smooth ball forms. Remove dough and finish kneading by hand. Place in a greased bowl and cover. Let rise until doubled in bulk, about 1 hour.

Place dough on floured surface and roll into large square. Place on vegetable oil sprayed cookie sheet and cover. Let rise another ½ hour. Brush dough with a little olive oil and sprinkle with additional herbs. Rosemary is nice. Bake at 400°F (200°C) about 20 minutes.

Makes

1 large loaf

Variations

To make **Sage Focaccia**, substitute ½ cup (125 mL) chopped fresh sage for the basil, thyme and oregano. Omit the pepper. Proceed as above. After brushing dough with olive oil, press fresh sage leaves into dough and sprinkle with coarse salt (optional). Bake as above.

To make **Rosemary Olive Focaccia**, substitute 1 tbsp. (15 mL) minced fresh rosemary for the basil, thyme and oregano. Proceed as above. After brushing dough with olive oil, sprinkle with ½ cup (125 mL) Parmesan cheese and press into dough. Bake at 400°F (200°C) for 15 minutes. Coarsely chop 6 Kalamata olives, 4 oil-packed sun-dried tomatoes and 2 large garlic cloves, and arrange over bread. Sprinkle lightly with Parmesan cheese. Drizzle 1 tbsp. (15 mL) olive oil over. Top with fresh rosemary sprigs and bake 5-10 minutes, until cheese melts.

Onion Flatbread

1 tbsp.	yeast (7 g env.)	15 mL
1 tbsp.	sugar	15 mL
¼ cup	warm water (105-115°F [40-45°C])	60 mL
1 cup	warm water (as above)	250 mL
6 tbsp.	butter, melted and cooled	90 mL
¼ cup	plain yogurt	60 mL
1	egg, beaten to blend	1
2 tsp.	salt	10 mL
4½ cups	all-purpose flour (or more)	1.25 L
2 tsp.	baking powder	10 mL
	vegetable oil	
2 tbsp.	butter	30 mL
¾ cup	minced onions	175 mL
	poppy seeds	

Method

Sprinkle yeast and sugar over ¼ cup (60 mL) water in medium bowl; stir to dissolve. Let stand until foamy, 5 minutes.

Stir 1 cup (250 mL) water, melted butter, yogurt, egg and salt into yeast mixture. Add 2 cups (500 mL) flour and baking powder and beat until smooth. Mix in enough of remaining flour 1 cup (250 mL) at a time to form a soft dough. Turn out onto floured surface and knead until smooth and elastic, 10-12 minutes. Oil large bowl. Add dough, turning to coat entire surface. Cover bowl. Let dough rise in draft-free area until doubled (1½ hours).

Meanwhile, melt 2 tbsp. (30 mL) butter in skillet over medium heat. Add onions and cook until golden, stirring occasionally, about 15 minutes. Cool. Grease baking sheets. Punch down dough and knead on lightly floured surface until smooth. Divide into 12 pieces. Shape one piece into a round. (Keep remainder covered to prevent drying). Press 1/12 of onions into center. Pull dough up and over onions, pinching to close. Pat dough into 6" (15 cm) disc. Place on baking sheet, seam side down. Brush with oil. Sprinkle with poppy seeds. Cover. Repeat with remaining dough pieces. Let breads rise in warm draft-free area until puffy, about 10 minutes.

Position rack in center of oven and preheat oven to 500°F (260°C). Bake flatbreads until puffed and beginning to brown, about 6 minutes. This can be prepared ahead. Cool, then wrap in foil. Store at room temperature 1 day or freeze up to 2 weeks. Reheat at 350°F (180°C). Serve warm.

Makes 12

Sun-Dried Tomato Poppyseed Flatbread

This is a great accompaniment to a Greek or Mediterranean dinner.

1 tbsp.	yeast (7 g env.)	15 mL
1 tsp.	honey	5 mL
½ cup	warm water	125 mL
1¼ cups	flour	300 mL
⅓ cup	rye or whole-wheat flour	75 mL
4 tbsp.	melted butter	60 mL
3 tbsp.	poppy seeds	45 mL
1 tsp.	salt	5 mL
	cornmeal	
1	garlic clove, minced	1
½ cup	chopped green onion	125 mL
1 cup	chopped sun-dried tomatoes in oil	250 mL
	salt	
	butter	

Method   Dissolve yeast and honey in warm water. Combine flours, 1 tbsp. (15 mL) butter, poppy seeds and salt in processor. Running machine, add yeast and honey mixture and process about 30 seconds. If dough is too sticky add more flour; if too dry add warm water. Process until smooth and elastic. Put dough in large plastic bag and let rise until doubled. Heat oven to 450°F (230°C). Oil large cookie sheet, sprinkle with cornmeal. Roll dough to 10 x 12" (25 x 30 cm) rectangle. Transfer to pan. Combine remaining butter and garlic; brush over dough. Sprinkle green onion and sun-dried tomatoes on dough and gently press in. Sprinkle lightly with salt and bake about 15 minutes. Brush with butter again and cut in squares.

Makes   1 large flatbread

Homemade Herbed Boboli

*This focaccia-type bread puffs up so thick and spongy!
It makes an incredible pizza crust.*

2⅔ cups	water	650 mL
1 tbsp.	instant yeast (7 g env.)	15 mL
⅓ cup	oil	75 mL
1 tbsp.	sugar	15 mL
1 tbsp.	salt	15 mL
1 tbsp.	dried basil	15 mL
1 tbsp.	minced garlic	15 mL
1 tbsp.	dried oregano	15 mL
4 tbsp.	Parmesan cheese	60 mL
5-6 cups	flour	1.25-1.5 L
	olive oil	
	additional herbs or spices and	
	Parmesan cheese	

Method   In a large bowl mix first 9 ingredients. Stir in flour and knead until smooth and no longer sticky. Place in clean, oiled bowl and let rise 45 minutes. remove dough from bowl, punch down and let rest about 15-20 minutes. Push out flat on greased pizza pan. Brush with oil and sprinkle on additional herbs or spices (e.g., fresh rosemary or Cajun spice mix) and Parmesan cheese. Bake in oven at 410°F (210°C) about 30 minutes.

Makes   1 flatbread

Fresh Pita Bread

1 cup	warm water	250 mL
1 tbsp.	yeast, instant* or regular	15 mL
1 tsp.	sugar	5 mL
1 cup	cake flour	250 mL
2 cups	unbleached flour	500 mL
	salt	
1 tbsp.	oil	15 mL

Method

Combine water, yeast and sugar. Let stand 5-10 minutes. In processor, using steel knife, combine cake flour, 1½ cups bleached flour, salt and yeast. Process on and off.

Add remaining flour, processing on and off until dough is sticky but not wet. Add oil and process about 40 seconds.

Place in oiled bowl, making sure top of dough is properly greased. Cover with a damp towel and let rise about 1 hour, or until dough has doubled. Punch down and let rest 30 minutes. Preheat oven to 500°F (260°C).

Lightly flour board and place dough on floured board. Cut into 8 equal pieces. Roll each piece into a circle not more than 5" (13 cm) in diameter.

Place circle on greased cookie sheet. Bake about 8 minutes, until lightly browned. Do not overbake.

Makes

8 pitas

* If using instant yeast simply add to dry ingredients – omit standing time.

Sun-Dried Tomato Bagels

A great treat to make with your own sun-dried tomatoes, see page 55.
You can't buy bagels like these.

1 cup	milk	250 mL
¼ cup	butter	60 mL
1½ tbsp.	sugar	22 mL
1 tbsp.	instant yeast (7 g env.)	15 mL
1½ cups	flour	375 mL
4 oz.	sun-dried tomatoes*	115 g
1 tbsp.	chopped fresh basil	15 mL
1	egg, separated	1
1 tsp.	salt	5 mL
1 tsp.	water	5 mL
	sesame seeds, poppy seeds or	
	finely chopped sun-dried tomatoes	

Method
In microwave, heat milk and butter. Cool to lukewarm. In processor, blend sugar, yeast, flour, tomatoes and basil. Add egg white and milk mixture and process until smooth ball forms, adding more flour if dough is sticky. Cover with plastic on a floured surface and let rise about 1 hour.

Cut dough into 20-24 pieces and shape into rings. Set back on floured surface to rise further, about 10-15 minutes.

Meanwhile, bring a large pot of water to a boil with 1 tsp. (5 mL) salt. Place bagels in water and boil about 20 seconds, turning once. Place on greased baking sheet. Beat egg yolk with water and brush over bagels. Top with sesame seeds, poppy seeds or finely chopped sun-dried tomatoes. Bake at 400°F (200°C) about 20 minutes, until golden.

Makes
20-24 bagels

* If tomatoes are not packed in oil, soften in water in microwave for 1 minute on high or cover with boiling water and let stand for about ½ hour.

Holiday Dinner Rolls

This is a particularly easy recipe to prepare. There is very little kneading and the rising time is comparatively short.

2 tbsp.	instant yeast (7 g env.)	30 mL
7-8 cups	flour	1.75-2 L
2	eggs	2
½ cup	sugar	125 mL
6 tbsp.	vegetable oil	90 mL
3 cups	lukewarm water	750 mL
2 tsp.	salt	10 mL

Glaze:

| 1 | egg | 1 |
| 1 tsp. | water | 5 mL |

Toppings:

Parmesan cheese
poppy seeds
sesame seeds
sifted flour
cornmeal

Method   Mix yeast and 4 cups (1 L) of the flour. In a separate bowl, whip eggs, sugar, oil and water.

Add flour/yeast mixture; blend well. Add salt and enough of remaining flour to make a workable dough. Let rise 15 minutes. Punch down. Form into 4-5 dozen buns. Place in greased pans.

Glaze: Beat egg with water and brush over unrisen buns.

Toppings: Top buns with one or all of the toppings. Cover and let rise on kitchen counter or a warm place for 1 hour. Bake in 350°F (180°C) oven for 15-18 minutes.

Makes   4-5 dozen

Pictured on page 87.

Pesto French Bread

½ cup	pesto (see page 107)	125 mL
¼ cup	freshly grated Parmesan cheese	60 mL
1 scant tbsp.	yeast (7 g env.)	15 mL
1 cup	plus 2 tbsp. lukewarm water	280 mL
1 tbsp.	safflower oil	15 mL
2 tsp.	salt	10 mL
2 cups	whole-wheat flour	500 mL
2 cups	unbleached white flour, plus additional for kneading	500 mL
	cornmeal (optional)	

Method

First make the pesto. Stir in the additional Parmesan.

Dissolve the yeast in the water and let sit for 10 minutes. Stir in the pesto and combine thoroughly. Add the safflower oil and salt, and fold in the whole-wheat flour. Stir in the unbleached white flour and turn the dough onto a lightly floured surface.

Knead for 10 minutes, or until dough is smooth and elastic. This can also be done in a mixer. Shape into a ball.

Place dough in lightly oiled bowl, turning to coat entire surface. Position seam side down. Cover and let rise in a warm place for about 1½ hours, or until doubled in bulk.

Punch down dough and divide into 2 equal pieces. Knead each piece briefly and shape into a tight round loaf. If you are going to bake on baking stones, first place dough on a baking sheet sprinkled with cornmeal; otherwise place it on an oiled baking sheet sprinkled with cornmeal. Cover and let rise in a warm place for 45 minutes to 1 hour, until doubled in bulk.

Preheat the oven to 450°F (230°C). If using baking stones, heat the stones in oven for 30 minutes and sprinkle with cornmeal just before you slide the loaves onto them. Slash the loaves with a razor blade or a sharp knife and slide them onto the hot stones, or, if using a baking sheet, place this in the oven. Turn heat down to 400°F (200°C) and spray loaves with water 3 times in the first 10 minutes. Bake 40 minutes, until loaves are a deep brown color and respond to tapping with a hollow thumping sound. Remove and cool on a rack.

Makes

2 loaves

Sourdough French Processor Bread

Unbelievable! Form into one gigantic loaf.

2 cups	flour (approx.)	500 mL
2 tsp.	salt	10 mL
1 tbsp.	yeast (7 g env.)	15 mL
1 tsp.	sugar	5 mL
½ cup	warm water	125 mL
1 cup	Sourdough Starter (below)	250 mL
¼ cup	flour	60 mL

Method   In processor bowl put flour and salt; mix. Dissolve yeast in sugar and warm water. Add yeast mixture to flour with sourdough starter. Process on and off. If too sticky add flour; if too dry add water. Process on and off until well kneaded. Take out dough, knead a bit by hand until smooth. Place in a greased bowl and let rise about 50 minutes. Form dough into a long loaf, slashing across the top. Let rise ½ hour longer. Sift ¼ cup (60 mL) flour across top and bake at 375°F (190°C) about 1 hour.

Makes   1 loaf

Pictured on page 51.

Sourdough Starter

Start this 3 days ahead.

Starter:

2 cups	flour	500 mL
2 cups	warm water	500 mL
1 tsp.	salt	5 mL
3 tbsp.	sugar	45 mL
1 tbsp.	yeast	15 mL

To renew:

1 cup	flour	250 mL
1 cup	warm water	250 mL

Method   Combine starter ingredients in bowl. Stir well. Cover and leave on shelf for 3 days, stirring a few times each day. A few hours before baking bread, take 1 cup (250 mL) of this mixture and place in a bowl with 1 cup (250 mL) flour and 1 cup (250 mL) warm water. Stir. Take out 1 cup (250 mL) for the above recipe. Add remainder to original starter recipe and store in refrigerator.

Cheddar Cheese Bread Processor Style

1 tbsp.	yeast (7 g env.)	15 mL
¼ cup	warm water	60 mL
1 tbsp.	sugar	15 mL
3 oz.	Cheddar cheese, grated (¾ cup [175 mL])	85 g
3 cups	flour	750 mL
1 tsp.	salt	5 mL
¼ cup	chilled butter	60 mL
½ cup	warm milk	125 mL
1	egg	1
2 tbsp.	cornmeal	30 mL

Glaze:

1	egg	1
1 tbsp.	cream	15 mL
	sesame seeds	

Method Dissolve yeast in warm water with sugar. Grate cheese into work bowl of food processor. Add flour and salt. Process on and off. Add butter, 1 tbsp. (15 mL) at a time. Process on and off. Add yeast, milk and egg. Process until a ball forms. If too dry, add warm water; if too sticky add flour. Remove dough, divide into 8 pieces*. Put back in work bowl and process 15 seconds. Remove dough and knead 2-3 minutes. Place dough in a buttered bowl, cover and let rise until doubled in bulk, about 45-60 minutes. When risen, punch down, form into a loaf. Place on greased sheet dusted with cornmeal. Cover and let rise again until doubled, 45-60 minutes. Brush with egg and cream beaten together and sprinkle with sesame seeds. Bake at 400°F (200°C) 35-40 minutes.

Makes 1 loaf

*Dividing the dough gives the processor a chance to break it down more completely and knead it more thoroughly.

Garlic Cheese Bread

1 tbsp.	yeast (7 g env.)	15 mL
1 tsp.	sugar	5 mL
1 cup	warm water	250 mL
1 cup	cake flour	250 mL
2¼ cups	white flour	550 mL
1½ tsp.	salt	7 mL
2 tbsp.	soft butter	30 mL
1	egg	1

Garlic Cheese Filling:

1	large garlic clove	1
1	shallot	1
4 oz.	Parmesan cheese	125 g
4 oz.	Mozzarella cheese	125 g
¼ cup	chopped parsley	60 mL
1	egg	1

Glaze:

| 1 | egg | 1 |
| 1 tsp. | salt | 5 mL |

Method Dissolve yeast and sugar in warm water. In processor, mix flours and salt. Add dissolved yeast, butter and egg. Process on and off until a soft ball forms. You may have to add more flour. Remove dough and knead a few minutes. Place in a greased bowl, covered with a damp cloth, and let rise until doubled.

While dough is rising, prepare the filling. Mince garlic and shallot in a food processor. Add cheese cut in small pieces. Add parsley and egg. Process well.

When risen, roll dough into 8 x 16" (20 x 41 cm) rectangle. Cover evenly with filling. Roll loaf into a jelly roll, pinching seams to seal. Place on a greased baking sheet. Slash loaf 3 or 4 times. Let rise again about 30 minutes. Brush loaf with an egg, beaten with 1 tsp. (5 mL) salt. Bake at 375°F (190°C) for 30-35 minutes.

Makes 1 loaf

Almond–Chive Bread

1 tbsp.	yeast	15 mL
1 tbsp.	honey	15 mL
1 cup	warm water (98°F [37°C])	250 mL
½ cup	chopped almonds	125 mL
1 cup	whole-wheat pastry flour	250 mL
2 cups	unbleached flour	500 mL
2 tbsp.	minced fresh chives	30 mL
1 tsp.	salt	5 mL

Method In a large bowl, combine the yeast, honey and 1½ cups (375 mL) of water. Let the bowl stand in a warm spot until the yeast mixture bubbles, about 10 minutes.

In a blender, combine the almonds and remaining ½ cup (125 mL) water. Purée, then strain through a fine sieve. Add the almond liquid to the yeast mixture; reserve the solids.

Stir the pastry flour and ½ cup (125 mL) of the unbleached flour into the yeast mixture. Mix well with a wooden spoon. Let this batter rise in a warm place for 30 minutes.

Stir in the reserved almonds, chives, salt substitute, and enough of the remaining flour to form a kneadable dough.

Turn onto a lightly floured surface and knead for 5-8 minutes, or until the dough becomes elastic and less sticky. Place in a clean, lightly oiled bowl. Cover and let rise in a warm, draft-free place for 1 hour. Punch down and let rise again for 30 minutes. Preheat oven to 350°F (180°C).

Lightly oil a large baking sheet. Form a large round loaf from the dough and place in the center of the sheet.

Bake for 45-60 minutes, or until the loaf is golden and sounds slightly hollow when you tap it on the top. Transfer to a wire rack to cool before slicing.

Makes 1 loaf

Tomato Herb Bread

3 cups	warm water (98-110°F [37-42°C])	750 mL
2 tbsp.	honey	30 mL
1 tbsp.	yeast (7 g env.)	15 mL
6-7 cups	whole-wheat flour	1.5-1.75 L
½ cup	drained and diced, oil-packed, sun-dried tomatoes	125 mL
¼ cup	olive oil	60 mL
1 tbsp.	tomato paste	15 mL
2 tsp.	salt	10 mL

Method   In a large bowl combine the water, honey and yeast. Let stand in warm place until the mixture foams, about 10 minutes. Stir in 2 cups (500 mL) flour, mixing well with a wooden spoon. Let this batter rise in a warm place for 30 minutes.

Stir in the tomatoes, oil, tomato paste, salt substitute and enough flour to make a kneadable dough.

Turn onto lightly floured surface and knead for 5-8 minutes, or until the dough becomes elastic and less sticky. Place in a clean lightly oiled bowl. Cover and let rise again for 30 minutes. Lightly oil 2, 5 x 9" (13 x 23 cm) loaf pans. Divide the dough in half, form each half into a loaf and place in the pans. Let rise for 20 minutes.

Preheat oven to 375°F (190°C). Bake the loaves for 40 minutes, or until lightly browned. Turn out onto wire racks and let cool before slicing.

Makes   2 loaves

Basic Biscuit Mix

9 cups	flour	2 L
5 tbsp.	baking powder	60 mL
1 tbsp.	salt	15 mL
1½ tbsp.	sugar	22 mL
1 lb.	shortening, cold	500 g

Method   Combine dry ingredients and cut shortening into dry mixture until texture is like coarse crumbs. Store covered in a cool dry place.

Makes   about 10 cups (2.5 L) of mix

Variation   **Herbed Biscuit Mix:** For variety add 1-2 tbsp. (15-30 mL) dried mixed herbs, chives, basil, oregano, etc.

Mediterranean Tomato Bread with Olive Butter

1 tbsp.	instant yeast	15 mL
2 cups	warm milk	500 mL
7 cups	biscuit mix (see page 46)	1.75 L
¼ cup	sugar	60 mL
½ tsp.	salt	2 mL
4	large eggs	4
¼ tsp.	cream of tartar	1 mL
½ cup	chopped sun-dried tomatoes	125 mL
2 tbsp.	minced garlic	30 mL
¼ cup	Parmesan cheese	60 mL
2 tbsp.	chopped fresh basil	30 mL
	melted butter	
	Parmesan cheese	

Method Sprinkle yeast over warm milk. Mix dry ingredients in large bowl. Whisk eggs, milk mixture and cream of tartar in a small bowl. Add to dry ingredients with remaining ingredients, stirring until well blended. Cover with plastic wrap. Let rise in warm place until doubled in size, about 45 minutes. Stir dough down and pour into 2 well-greased 9 x 5" (23 x 13 cm) loaf pans. Cover with plastic wrap and let rise again about 1 hour.

Preheat oven to 350°F (180°C). Brush loaves with a bit of melted butter and sprinkle with additional Parmesan cheese. Bake about 40 minutes. Serve bread with the Olive Butter (below).

Makes 1 loaf

Olive Butter

½ cup	butter, softened	125 mL
1	garlic clove	1
½ cup	pitted Greek black olives	125 mL
¼ cup	fresh parsley	60 mL

Method In a processor blend butter, garlic, black olives and parsley. Process until fluffy.

Makes about 1 cup (250 mL)

End of Summer Herb Bread

This is a light and airy "I can't believe you made this" type of bread where you decide on which wonderful herb flavor to feature. Why not throw in a cup of finely chopped sun-dried tomatoes (add to the dry ingredients).

3 cups	flour	750 mL
2 tbsp.	sugar	30 mL
2 tsp.	salt	10 mL
1 tbsp.	instant yeast	15 mL
¼ cup	chopped mixed fresh herbs (basil, thyme, rosemary, chives)	60 mL
3 tbsp.	Parmesan cheese	45 mL
1½ cups	(approx.) warm chicken or vegetable broth	375 mL
2 tbsp.	light margarine, melted additional chopped herbs	30 mL

Method

In a food processor, mix flour, sugar, salt, yeast, herbs and cheese. Slowly add warm (not hot) stock, using only enough to make a soft dough. Process about 5 minutes. Dough should not be sticky. Remove from processor and knead by hand to form a smooth ball. Place in an oiled bowl, cover and let rise in warm place until doubled, about 45 minutes.

Form dough into a round loaf or whatever shape you wish. Brush with melted margarine and top with herbs. Place on an oiled cookie sheet, cover and let rise again until doubled.

Preheat oven to 375°F (190°C). Bake loaf for 30-40 minutes. Remove from oven and brush again with melted margarine.

Makes 1 loaf

Shredded Wheat Bread

The ultimate!

3	shredded wheat biscuits	3
⅓ cup	fancy molasses	75 mL
⅓ cup	sugar	75 mL
2 tsp.	salt	10 mL
3 tbsp.	butter	45 mL
2 cups	boiling water	500 mL
2 tbsp.	instant or regular yeast (2, 7 g env.)	30 mL
1 tsp.	sugar	5 mL
4-6 cups	flour	1-1.5 L

Shredded Wheat Bread
Continued

Method Place shredded wheat, molasses, sugar, salt and butter in large bowl. Add boiling water; stir. Let sit about 30 minutes, until completely cool. Meanwhile, combine yeast and sugar. Stir yeast mixture into cooled shredded wheat mixture. Add enough flour to make a soft dough. Knead until smooth and elastic, about 5-10 minutes. Place in a large greased bowl, turn to grease top and cover. Let rise until doubled. Form dough into 2 loaves, in pans or in French bread shape. Let rise until doubled. Bread should not be sticky. Bake at 375°F (190°C) for approximately 25-30 minutes. Serve with Mango Butter (page 50).

Makes 2 loaves

Herbed Cottage Cheese Loaf
This is the puffiest, lightest bread.

1 cup	cottage cheese, warmed	250 mL
2 tbsp.	sugar	30 mL
3 tbsp.	minced fresh green onions	45 mL
1 tsp.	dillweed	5 mL
1 tsp.	salt	5 mL
1½ tbsp.	butter	22 mL
1 tsp.	dried thyme	5 mL
1 tsp.	dried oregano	5 mL
¼ tsp.	baking soda	1 mL
1	egg	1
1 tbsp.	yeast (1, 7 g env.)	15 mL
¼ cup	warm water	60 mL
2½-2¾ cups	flour	625-675 mL
	melted butter	
	Parmesan cheese	

Method Combine the first 10 ingredients in large bowl. Dissolve yeast in water. Add yeast to large bowl and mix at medium for 30 seconds. Add flour. Finish mixing with hands until dough is stiff and well blended. Microwave on medium low for 1 minute. Be sure to place a cup of water in the microwave for moisture. Cover and let rise 45 minutes. Punch down and turn into well-greased 8" (20 cm) round ovenproof dish (try a springform pan). Cover, let rise about 45 minutes. Bake at 350°F (180°C) for 40-50 minutes. Brush top with melted butter and sprinkle with Parmesan cheese.

Makes 1 loaf

Sunflower Seed Bread

Form this into a big sunflower. It looks dramatic and tastes even better.

2 tbsp.	instant yeast	30 mL
1 tbsp.	sugar	15 mL
2 cups	whole-wheat flour	500 mL
2 cups	all-purpose flour	500 mL
1½ tsp.	salt	7 mL
1¾ cups	warm water	425 mL
2 tbsp.	oil	30 mL
¾ cup	shelled sunflower seeds	175 mL
1	egg, beaten	1
	poppy seeds	
	additional sunflower seeds	

Method   In food processor, blend dry ingredients. Add warm water, oil and sunflower seeds and process until a smooth round of dough is formed, adding more flour or water if needed. Place dough in oiled bowl and cover with plastic wrap. Let rise in warm place until doubled in bulk, about 1 hour.

When dough has risen, punch down and form into 1 large round and 6 small rounds. Place large round in center of well-oiled cookie sheet. Place small rounds around large round. Brush dough with egg. Sprinkle small rounds with sunflower seeds. Cover with plastic wrap and let rise in warm place about 45 minutes. Preheat oven to 375°F (190°C). Bake loaf, 45 minutes to 1 hour, until golden brown. Serve with Mango Butter (below), if desired.

Makes   1 loaf

Mango Butter

½ cup	butter	125 mL
1 cup	drained mango slices	250 mL

Method   Cream butter in food processor; add mango and process until smooth.

Makes   about 1 cup (250 mL)

Soup and Bread

Condiments

Garlic Red Pepper Rouille

Pronounced roo-EE, this traditional French-Mediterranean sauce is basically a garlic mayonnaise enriched with saffron and finely ground cayenne pepper. It is a wonderful accompaniment to vegetable and fish soups, a fish bouillabaisse is traditional and the Bouillabaisse of Vegetables on page 56 is also more flavorful garnished with rouille.

6	large fresh garlic cloves	6
2	large egg yolks, at room temperature	2
1 cup	extra-virgin olive oil	250 mL
¼ tsp.	saffron threads	1 mL
	finely ground cayenne pepper, to taste	
1	red pepper, roasted and peeled	1

Method   Peel the garlic cloves and cut in ½. If there is a green sprout that runs lengthwise through the center of the garlic, remove it.

In a food processor, process garlic cloves and egg yolks until thick and creamy. Add oil through feed tube, slowly until thickened. Add saffron and cayenne pepper. To intensify color and flavor add a roasted, peeled red pepper at this point and purée until smooth. Taste the rouille and add additional cayenne, if desired. Cover and refrigerate until ready to serve.

Makes   about 1¼ cups (300 mL)

Pictured on page 51.

Chunky Almond Dressing

1 cup	slivered almonds	250 mL
¼ cup	butter	60 mL
⅓ cup	lemon juice	75 mL
1 tbsp.	chopped fresh basil	15 mL
3 tbsp.	honey	45 mL
1 cup	oil	250 mL
3 tbsp.	Dijon mustard	45 mL
1 tsp.	chopped fresh oregano	5 mL

Method   In 300°F (150°C) oven, lightly toast almonds in butter. Cool slightly. Put remaining ingredients in blender and blend well. Add almonds and blend on and off until chunky. Serve over butter lettuce.

Makes   about 3 cups (750 mL)

Sun-Dried Tomatoes Homestyle

I love to go to the local produce market and buy a big bag of marked-down tomatoes for this. My first choice would be Roma tomatoes because of their compact size for slicing and their low juice content.

12 or more	ripe tomatoes	12 or more
	salt	

Method   Slice tomatoes quite thin and blot with paper towel. Spread on cookie sheets lined with foil and sprayed with nonstick vegetable oil. Sprinkle lightly with salt and place in oven set at 200°F (100°C). Leave overnight. Tomatoes will be dried by morning. Remove from foil and store in a jar of garlic olive oil or rosemary oil or simply store in a plastic bag in the refrigerator. Oven temperatures may vary depending on how accurate your oven is.

Tomato-Basil Butter

½ cup	softened butter	125 mL
½ cup	sun-dried tomatoes	125 mL
2 tbsp.	chopped fresh basil	30 mL

Method   Process or whip all ingredients together until fluffy.
Makes   about 1 cup (250 mL)

Lemon-Chive Butter

Although this butter is meant to be spread on biscuits, it is also splendid on toast, baked potatoes, roast chicken and pasta.

6 tbsp.	chopped fresh parsley	90 mL
2 tbsp.	snipped fresh tarragon	30 mL
3 tbsp.	snipped chives	45 mL
1 tsp.	grated lemon peel	5 mL
2 cups	unsalted butter	500 mL
1 tbsp.	fresh lemon juice	15 mL
	salt to taste	

Method   Finely mince herbs and lemon peel in food processor, scraping sides of bowl often. Add butter, lemon juice and salt and blend well. Turn into a crock. Cover tightly and chill overnight or for up to 3 days. Let stand at room temperature 30 minutes before serving.
Makes   about 2¼ cups (550 mL)

Cranberry Butter

The ultimate holiday spread for your favorite holiday breads!

¾ cup	cranberries	175 mL
6 tbsp.	powdered sugar	90 mL
2 tsp.	grated lemon peel	10 mL
1 cup	unsalted butter, at room temperature, cut into pieces	250 mL

Method   Coarsely chop cranberries with sugar and lemon peel in processor using on/off turns. Add butter and blend until mixture is combined but slightly chunky.

Note   This can be prepared 1 week ahead. Cover and refrigerate. Bring to room temperature before serving.

Makes   about 1½ cups (375 mL)

Cranberry-Kumquat Relish

This refreshing condiment has a bonus to its terrific flavors – it's uncooked and can be made 2 days ahead, making it a big time saver during a busy season.

2 x 12 oz.	pkgs. fresh cranberries	2 x 340 g
20	kumquats or 2 small oranges, cut into 1" (2.5 cm) pieces	20
2 cups	sugar	500 mL
½ cup	dried currants	125 mL

Method   Place fresh cranberries, kumquats and sugar in processor. Process fruit mixture until finely chopped, using on/off turns. Transfer relish to medium bowl. Mix in dried currants. Let stand at room temperature at least 1 hour. This can be prepared 2 days ahead. Cover and refrigerate. Serve cold or at room temperature.

Makes   about 5 cups (1.25 L)

Pictured on page 87.

Cranberry-Rhubarb Relish

Ginger and lemon add zest to this colorful relish.

4 cups	fresh cranberries (1½ x 12 oz. [340 g] bags)	1 L
20 oz.	pkg. frozen rhubarb	625 g
2 cups	sugar	500 mL
1 cup	water	250 mL
1 cup	chopped crystallized ginger	250 mL
¼ cup	minced lemon peel	60 mL

Method Combine all ingredients in large heavy saucepan. Cook over medium-low heat until sugar dissolves, stirring occasionally. Increase heat and boil until cranberries pop, about 10 minutes. Remove from heat. Cover and let stand 15 minutes. Cover and refrigerate until well chilled

Note This can be prepared 1 week ahead.

Makes about 4 cups (1 L)

Mango Salsa

1 cup	diced ripe mango	250 mL
⅓ cup	diced red pepper	75 mL
¼ cup	diced cucumber	60 mL
3 tbsp.	finely chopped scallions	45 mL
1 tbsp.	fresh lime juice	15 mL
1 tbsp.	tomato purée	15 mL
¼ tsp.	dried hot red pepper flakes	1 mL
	salt	

Method Combine all ingredients in a mixing bowl. Mix together with a fork, lightly mashing the mango. Turn into a serving bowl, cover and chill until ready to serve.

Makes   about 1¾ cup (422 mL)

Sweet Potato Mango Chutney

2	large sweet potatoes, peeled and diced	2
2 x 14 oz.	cans mango, drained	2 x 398 mL
2 cups	brown sugar	500 mL
2 cups	raisins	500 mL
3 tbsp.	chopped candied ginger	45 mL
2	large onions, chopped	2
1 tbsp.	cinnamon	15 mL
2	large green apples, chopped	2

Method Combine all ingredients in a large pot and bring to a boil. Reduce heat and simmer with lid on for about ½ hour. Serve at room temperature. This can be packed in hot sterilized jars and processed, otherwise it will keep about 2 weeks in the refrigerator.

Makes about 6 cups (1.5 L)

Plum Sauce

A perfect dip for spicy phyllos!

1 cup	plum preserves	250 mL
1	garlic clove	1
3 tbsp.	white wine	45 mL
1 tbsp.	Dijon mustard	15 mL
1 tsp.	dry mustard	5 mL

Method Mix all the ingredients in small saucepan. Heat the mixture over a low flame, just to melt the preserves.

Makes about 1 cup (250 mL)

Soups

Bouillabaisse of Vegetables

The original version is a seafood stew from Provence. This creative vegetarian adaptation is colorful and zesty.

2 tbsp.	olive oil	30 mL
2	medium onions, chopped	2
4	garlic cloves, whole, peeled	4
½ tsp.	saffron	2 mL
½ cup	fresh basil leaves	125 mL
1 cup	finely chopped fresh parsley	250 mL
½ tsp.	dried thyme	2 mL
½ tsp.	dried oregano	2 mL
2 tbsp.	tomato paste	30 mL
3 cups	dry white wine	750 mL
3 cups	water	750 mL
8	carrots, peeled, thickly sliced	8
4	potatoes, peeled, cut in chunks	4
4-6	celery stalks, chopped	4-6
1	medium zucchini, sliced	1
1	fennel bulb, quartered, sliced	1
1	broccoli head, separated into florets	1
4	tomatoes, peeled and halved	4
	freshly ground pepper and salt to taste	
	rouille (recipe follows) and garlic toast	

Method In a large kettle, heat the oil and sauté the onions until golden. Add the garlic, saffron, basil, parsley, thyme, oregano, tomato paste, wine, water, carrots and potatoes. Stir well and cover. Cook over medium heat for 8 minutes, then add the celery, zucchini and fennel, and continue cooking for another 8 minutes. Add the broccoli and tomatoes, then cook for an additional 4 minutes. Season with salt and pepper to taste. Serve.

Stir 2 tbsp. (30 mL) rouille into bouillabaisse. To serve, place vegetables in individual soup plates and then ladle over some soup liquid. Place 2-3 garlic toasts around the plates and top with a dollop of rouille. Pass the bowl of rouille for additional servings.

Serves 8

Variation Try Orange Rouille, page 61, or Garlic Red Pepper Rouille, page 54, for a colorful and flavorful change of pace.

Pictured on page 51.

Rouille

The traditional rouille is rich with egg yolks. This version is cholesterol-free and rivals the original in both taste and effect.

4	slices whole-wheat bread, soaked in water and squeezed dry	4
8	garlic cloves, peeled	8
1 tbsp.	tomato paste	15 mL
1 tbsp.	water	15 mL
¾ cup	olive oil	175 mL
¾ cup	tomato juice	175 mL
1 tsp.	cayenne pepper	5 mL
½ cup	chopped fresh parsley	125 mL

Method In a food processor, purée bread, garlic, tomato paste and water. While the processor is running, add olive oil slowly, through the feed tube, until you have a mayonnaise consistency. Add cayenne and parsley.

Makes about 1 cup (250 mL)

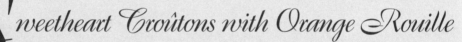

Sweetheart Croûtons with Orange Rouille

Cut bread into heart shapes for a special Valentine presentation. The extra rouille will keep for 1 week in the refrigerator. It is delicious spooned over vegetables or as a dip for crudités.

Orange Rouille:

7 oz.	jar roasted red peppers, drained and rinsed	200 g
1	garlic clove, minced	1
¾ tsp.	grated orange peel	3 mL
½ tsp.	salt	2 mL
⅛ tsp.	cayenne pepper	0.5 mL
⅛ tsp.	fennel seeds, crushed	0.5 mL
1	egg yolk	1
½ cup	olive oil	125 mL
4 x ½"	thick slices Italian or French bread	4 x 1.3 cm

Method Chop roasted peppers in processor with next 5 ingredients. Add yolk and purée until smooth. With machine running, gradually add oil through feed tube. This can be prepared 1 week ahead. Cover and refrigerate.

Preheat broiler. Broil bread until golden brown on both sides. Spread 1 side generously with rouille. Broil to heat through, about 30 seconds.

Makes 4 croûtons

Roasted Carrot and Brie Soup

Lighten up by using skimmed evaporated milk in place of heavy cream.

12	carrots, peeled and sliced	12
	butter	
	salt and pepper to taste	
2	onions	2
2 tbsp.	butter	30 mL
4 cups	chicken stock	1 L
8 oz.	Brie cheese, cut in pieces	250 g
1 cup	heavy cream	250 mL
	freshly ground coarse pepper	
	toasted almonds	

Method
Roast carrots, butter, salt and pepper in 425°F (220°C) oven for 20 minutes. Meanwhile sauté onions in 2 tbsp. (30 mL) butter until tender.

Heat chicken stock. Add onions and roasted carrots. Process or blend until smooth. Heat carrot mixture. Add Brie pieces. Stir until melted. Do not boil. Add heavy cream and pepper. Serve sprinkled with toasted almonds.

Serves   6-8

Golden Pepper Bisque

2	large yellow peppers	2
1 tbsp.	oil	15 mL
1	large onion	1
2	large potatoes, peeled, cut in ½" (1.3 cm) chunks	2
2	large carrots, peeled, sliced	2
1	celery stalk, chopped	1
6 cups	chicken stock	1.5 L
	olive oil	
	Parmesan cheese	
	salt and pepper	
	croûtons	

Golden Pepper Bisque

Continued

Method Broil or char peppers until black. Place in paper bag and cool. Peel peppers and cut into chunks.

Heat oil in large, heavy pan. Add onion and sauté until golden. Add peppers, potatoes, carrots, celery and broth. Simmer about 20 minutes. In blender or processor, purée vegetable mixture, a portion at a time. Reheat. Serve with a drizzle of olive oil, a sprinkle of cheese, salt, pepper and croûtons.

Serves 4-6

Puréed Artichoke Heart Soup with Walnuts

10 ½ oz.	can artichoke hearts*, drained well and excess liquid pressed out with paper towels	284 mL
1 cup	chicken stock	250 mL
1-2 tsp.	fresh lemon juice, or to taste	5-10 mL
¼ cup	heavy cream	60 mL
	freshly ground white pepper to taste	
	salt to taste	
½ cup	chopped walnuts	125 mL
2 tbsp.	unsalted butter	30 mL

Method In a saucepan, combine the artichoke hearts, broth, and lemon juice. Bring to a boil and simmer for 15 minutes. Purée the mixture in a blender or food processor and strain it through a fine sieve, pressing hard on the solids, into the pan. Stir in the cream, pepper and salt to taste and simmer the soup for 5 minutes. In a small skillet cook the walnuts in the butter over moderate heat, stirring, until they are golden. Ladle the soup into 2 heated bowls and sprinkle it with the walnuts.

Makes about 2½ cups (625 mL), serves 2

* Do not use marinated artichoke hearts for this recipe.

Cioppino

This U.S.-Italian version of bouillabaisse originated in San Francisco.

2 cups	chopped onion	500 mL
½ cup	chopped green pepper	125 mL
6	garlic cloves, minced	6
½ cup	olive oil	125 mL
35 oz.	can Italian tomatoes with basil	1 kg
5½ oz.	can tomato paste	156 mL
2 cups	red wine	500 mL
1	lemon, thinly sliced	1
1 cup	chopped parsley	250 mL
1 tsp.	dried basil	5 mL
1 tsp.	dried oregano	5 mL
1 tsp.	salt	5 mL
	freshly ground pepper	
	thyme to taste	
1½ lbs.	sea bass (or other similar white fish)*, cut in 2" (5 cm) pieces	750 g
3 x 1½ lb.	crabs, cut up	3 x 750 g
1 lb.	shrimp	500 g
12	hard-shelled clams*	12

Method Combine onion, green pepper and garlic with olive oil in large pot. Cook over low heat for 10 minutes. Stir occasionally. Add tomatoes and paste, wine, lemon, ½ cup (125 mL) parsley and all seasonings. Bring to a boil and then reduce heat. Cover and simmer 20 minutes. Add bass, crab and shrimp. Simmer, covered, 20 minutes more. Add clams. Simmer, covered, 10 minutes, or until clams open.

Serve in a black cast-iron pot. Sprinkle with remaining parsley.

Serves 8

* Seafood may be added or omitted according to taste. If fresh clams are not available substitute 5 oz. (142 g) baby clams with juice.

Seafood Bisque

6 cups	water	1.5 L
4	medium potatoes, peeled and quartered	4
2	medium onions, coarsely chopped	2
½	bay leaf	½
½ tsp.	dried thyme	2 mL
¼ tsp.	finely minced garlic	1 mL
1 tsp.	salt	5 mL
⅛ tsp.	freshly ground black pepper	0.5 mL
1 cup	chopped sea scallops, shrimp, lobster or crab meat (select one or more)	250 mL
2	egg yolks	2
½ cup	heavy cream	125 mL
	paprika	

Method Bring 2 cups (500 mL) of the water to boil. Add potatoes, onions, bay leaf, thyme, garlic, salt and pepper and simmer until the vegetables are barely tender, about 15 minutes. Add seafood during last 5 minutes of cooking.

Remove bay leaf and put mixture through sieve or blend to a purée. Return puréed mixture to saucepan and add remaining water. Bring to a boil and correct the seasonings.

Turn off heat and stir in egg yolks blended with cream. Serve hot or chilled. Garnish each serving with paprika.

Serves 8

Curried Chicken Soup with Applesauce

This undemanding soup is the ultimate comfort food for a bad cold or a down day. So smooth, it's slightly hot without being spicy.

¼ cup	cornstarch	60 mL
2-3 tsp.	curry powder	10-15 mL
4 cups	chicken stock	1 L
1 cup	applesauce	250 mL
½ cup	sour cream	125 mL
	apple slices, for garnish	

Method In a large saucepan stir together the cornstarch, curry powder and ½ cup (125 mL) of chicken stock. Add remaining stock and applesauce. Cook until thick and bubbly, stirring constantly. Reduce heat and cook 2 minutes longer. Remove from heat and slowly stir in sour cream. Garnish with apple slices.

Serves 4

Cream of Reuben Soup

If you love a Reuben sandwich, this soup is for you!

½ cup	beef stock	125 mL
½ cup	chicken stock	125 mL
¼ cup	chopped celery	60 mL
¼ cup	chopped onion	60 mL
1 tbsp.	cornstarch dissolved in	15 mL
2 tbsp.	water	30 mL
1 cup	chopped corned beef	250 mL
1 cup	chopped Swiss cheese	250 mL
¾ cup	sauerkraut, drained and rinsed	175 mL
¼ cup	butter	60 mL
2 cups	canned skim or 2% milk*	500 mL
	chives, for garnish	

Method Combine first 4 ingredients in large pan and bring to boil over high heat. Reduce heat and simmer until onion is tender crisp, about 5 minutes. Add dissolved cornstarch and cook until thick. Remove from heat and stir in corned beef, Swiss cheese and sauerkraut, blending well. Melt butter in pan; stir in milk. Add soup and blend well. Heat but do not boil. Garnish with chives.

Serves 8

* Canned milk is used because of its thicker consistency. It provides a creamy texture with much less fat.

Salads

Fruity Spinach Salad

Always a spectacular presentation, winter or summer! This fabulous dressing keeps indefinitely in the refrigerator.

Raspberry Poppyseed Dressing:

5 tbsp.	sugar	75 mL
4 tbsp.	raspberry vinegar	60 mL
1 tbsp.	minced onion	15 mL
1 tbsp.	poppyseeds	15 mL
1 tsp.	dry mustard	5 mL
½ cup	olive oil	125 mL

crisp spinach leaves, washed
kiwi slices
orange slices
strawberry slices

Method Mix all dressing ingredients, except oil, in blender for 1 minute. Slowly add oil and blend until thick. Arrange spinach on plates. Top with kiwi, orange and strawberry slices. Just before serving, drizzle with dressing.

Makes about 1 cup (250 mL) of dressing

Pictured on opposite page.

Spinach, Brie and Walnut Salad

¼ cup	olive oil	60 mL
1½ tbsp.	white wine vinegar	7 mL
	salt and pepper to taste	
8 cups	spinach leaves (about 6 oz. [170 g]), torn into bite-sized pieces	2 L
½ cup	thinly sliced red onion	125 mL
6 oz.	Brie cheese, diced, room temperature	170 g
2	sandwich-sized French bread slices	2
½ cup	toasted walnut pieces	125 mL
1	peach, sliced	1

Method Whisk oil and vinegar in small bowl. Season to taste with salt and pepper. Combine spinach, onion and half of cheese in large bowl. Preheat broiler. Divide remaining cheese between bread slices. Broil until cheese melts, about 1 minute. Cut toasts diagonally in half. Toss salad with enough dressing to coat well. Divide salad between 2 plates. Sprinkle with walnuts. Arrange 2 toast halves at edge of each salad and decorate with peach slices.

Serves 2

Salad and Bread

Fruity Spinach Salad with Raspberry Poppyseed Dressing, page 68
Danish Blue Herb Bread, page 7
Turquoise Margaritas, page 186

Spinach and Cashew Salad with Pear Vinaigrette

The cashews in this dressing add texture and wonderful flavor!

3	slices turkey bacon	3
7 cups	torn fresh spinach	6.75 L
1½ cups	sliced mushrooms	375 mL
2	green onions, sliced	2
2	oranges, peeled, thinly sliced	2
½ cup	diced purple onion	125 mL
½ cup	chopped cashews	125 mL

Pear Vinaigrette:

2	ripe pears, peeled, cored and diced	2
5 tbsp.	raspberry vinegar	75 mL
1 tbsp.	Dijon mustard	15 mL
¼ cup	roasted cashews	60 mL
½ cup	oil	125 mL
1 tsp.	dried oregano	5 mL
1 tsp.	dried thyme	5 mL
1 tsp.	coarsely ground black pepper	5 mL
1 tsp.	dried tarragon	5 mL

Method Cook turkey bacon until crispy. Blot dry and crumble into pieces. Arrange spinach on a large platter and top with mushrooms, onions, orange segments, purple onion and bacon. Drizzle with Pear Vinaigrette (below). Top with cashews.

Pear Vinaigrette: Blend all ingredients until smooth and creamy.

Serves 6-8

Variation Try Mango Chutney Dressing as an alternative to the Pear Vinaigrette.

Mango Chutney Dressing:

¼ cup	balsamic vinegar or	60 mL
3 tbsp.	red wine vinegar	45 mL
3 tbsp.	mango chutney	45 mL
1 tbsp.	sugar	15 mL
1	large garlic clove, chopped	1
1 tsp.	dry mustard	5 mL
⅓ cup	olive oil	75 mL

Method Combine vinegars, chutney, sugar, garlic and mustard in processor and blend well. With machine running, gradually add oil in thin steady stream. Blend until thickened. Season to taste with salt and pepper.

Makes about 1 cup (250 mL)

Mushroom and Pine Nut Salad with Raspberry Vinegar Dressing

Prepare this salad and toss with warm dressing just before serving.

	tender inner leaves of 1 head EACH curly endive, romaine and red leaf lettuce	
	tender inner leaves of 2 heads Boston or Bibb lettuce	
2	bunches watercress	2
¾ cup	walnut oil	175 mL
1 lb.	button mushrooms, Japanese tree mushrooms or wild mushrooms, cleaned trimmed and patted dry	500 g
¾ cup	pine nuts	175g
3½ oz.	pkg. enoki mushrooms	90 g
⅓ cup	raspberry vinegar	75 mL
	salt and freshly ground pepper	
8	small wedges of Brie (garnish)	8
	Basil Nectarine Flatbread (page 31)	

Method   Wash the lettuces and pat dry. Wash the watercress, stem and pat dry. Toss lettuce leaves and watercress in large bowl and set aside.

Heat ½ cup (125 mL) walnut oil in a large skillet over medium heat. Add button, Japanese or wild mushrooms and sauté until golden, about 5 minutes. Add pine nuts and cook until golden, about 5 minutes. Stir in Enoki mushrooms. Pour mushroom mixture over lettuce and toss.

Return skillet to medium heat, add remaining ¼ cup (60 mL) oil with raspberry vinegar, salt and pepper and mix well. Cook briefly to heat through. Pour over salad and toss again. Taste and adjust seasoning, adding more oil and vinegar as desired. Divide evenly among 8 serving plates. Garnish each with a wedge of Brie and some Basil Nectarine Flatbread. Serve salad warm.

Serves   6-8

Broccoli and Mushroom Salad

3 cups	broccoli florets	750 mL
2 tbsp.	crumbled crisp bacon	30 mL
½ cup	thinly sliced mushrooms	125 mL

Sour Cream Dressing:

½ cup	sour cream	125 mL
½ tsp.	freshly ground black pepper	2 mL
1	garlic clove, finely chopped	1
½ tsp.	Worcestershire sauce	2 mL
½ tsp.	salt	2 mL
	wine vinegar	

Method   Steam broccoli until tender-crisp; cool. In a large bowl, combine broccoli, bacon and mushrooms. In a small bowl combine sour cream, pepper, garlic, Worcestershire sauce, salt and vinegar. Mix well. Pour dressing over broccoli mixture. Toss gently. Refrigerate until serving time to chill thoroughly. Toss again before serving.

Serves   4

Tomato and Grilled Zucchini Salad

Get out the barbecue for this winner!

2 lbs.	medium-large zucchini, trimmed, halved lengthwise	1 kg
2 tbsp. + 1 cup	olive oil	280 mL
2 cups	fresh basil leaves	500 mL
3	garlic cloves, coarsely chopped	3
3 tbsp.	balsamic vinegar	45 mL
1 tbsp.	Dijon mustard	15 mL
	salt and pepper to taste	
2½ lbs.	large tomatoes, sliced	1.5 kg

Method   Heat barbecue to medium high. Position rack 6" (15 cm) above heat. Brush zucchini on all sides with 2 tbsp. (30 mL) oil. Grill until tender, turning occasionally, about 8 minutes. Transfer to plate and cool.

Purée basil, garlic, vinegar and mustard in processor. With machine running, add 1 cup (250 mL) oil; process until thick. Season with salt and pepper. Place tomatoes on platter. Cut zucchini into 1½" (4 cm) pieces. Mix zucchini and ¾ cup (175 mL) dressing. Spoon onto platter. Drizzle remaining dressing over tomatoes.

Serves   8

Middle Eastern Bread Salad

Try this simple salad as a light lunch or starter.
It's a savory accompaniment to roast leg of lamb or grilled fish.

4	pita bread rounds, torn into 1½-2" (4-5 cm) pieces	4
2	cucumbers, peeled, diced	2
2	tomatoes, peeled, diced	2
⅔ cup	drained canned chickpeas	150 mL
½ cup	fresh lemon juice	125 mL
½ cup	EACH chopped fresh mint leaves, cilantro and dillweed	125 mL
⅓ cup	extra virgin olive oil	75 mL
¼ cup	Kalamata olives	60 mL
6	romaine lettuce leaves, thinly sliced	6
3	green onions, thinly sliced	3
3	garlic cloves, finely chopped	3
1 tsp.	salt	5 mL
⅔ cup	plain yogurt	150 mL
3 tbsp.	fresh lemon zest	45 mL

Method   On baking sheet, bake pita bread at 400°F (200°C) for 5 minutes, until lightly toasted. Transfer to large bowl and cool. Add remaining ingredients, except yogurt and lemon zest, to bread and toss gently. Divide salad among 6 plates. Top with dollops of yogurt and lemon zest and serve.

Serves   6

Apple Spinach Slaw

2 tbsp.	mayonnaise	30 mL
2 tbsp.	plain yogurt or sour cream	30 mL
1 tbsp.	honey	15 mL
1 tsp.	Dijon mustard	5 mL
½ cup	chopped apple	125 mL
1 cup	coarsely chopped cabbage	250 mL
1 cup	coarsely chopped spinach	250 mL
2 tbsp.	chopped red onion	30 mL
	strawberries or orange slices (optional)	

Method   In a small bowl stir together the mayonnaise, yogurt, honey and mustard. Stir in apple. In a large bowl, combine cabbage, spinach and onion. Toss to mix. Add the first mixture and toss to coat. Garnish with strawberries or orange slices if desired.

Serves   2 -4

Caesar Salad To Live For

This version of the classic has almost no fat! Indulge!

1	head romaine lettuce	1

Nonfat Croûtons:

1 cup	French or sourdough bread cubes	250 mL
2	garlic cloves, minced	2
	seasoning salt or lemon pepper	
	reduced-fat Parmesan cheese	

Caesar Dressing To Live For:

3	large garlic cloves, minced	3
3	dashes Tabasco sauce	3
3	dashes Worcestershire sauce	3
2	egg whites	2
3 tbsp.	fresh lemon juice	45 mL
2 tbsp.	balsamic vinegar	30 mL
1 tbsp.	Dijon mustard	15 mL
½ cup	nonfat yogurt or nonfat sour cream	125 mL
	freshly ground pepper	
⅓ cup	reduced-fat Parmesan cheese	75 mL

Method Wash, dry and tear the lettuce leaves. Set aside

Nonfat Croûtons: Place bread cubes in a glass baking dish. Spray lightly with a baking spray. Add garlic, seasoning and cheese. Microwave on high about 4 minutes.

Dressing: In a large bowl, whisk first 7 ingredients well. Whisk in yogurt or sour cream and fresh pepper.

Add lettuce, Parmesan cheese and croûtons to dressing and toss well.

Serves 4-6

Sun-Dried Caesar Wedges

A salad or an appetizer? You decide or serve as a regular Caesar Salad.

1	egg	1
1 tbsp.	Dijon mustard	15 mL
⅓ cup	lemon juice	75 mL
	dash Tabasco sauce	
3	garlic cloves, quartered	3
⅓ cup	grated Parmesan cheese	75 mL
½ cup	sun-dried tomatoes	125 mL
1 cup	olive oil	250 mL
	chopped parsley	
	romaine lettuce or Belgian endive	
	croûtons and Parmesan cheese	
	for garnish	

Method Process first 7 ingredients. With processor on, slowly add olive oil. Stir in parsley. Cut romaine lettuce or Belgian endive into wedges and arrange on large platter. Drizzle dressing over and top with croûtons and more Parmesan cheese.

Serves 4-6

Caesar Salad with Tortellini and Asparagus

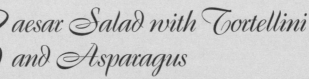

What a vegetarian meal or side dish!

4 cups	hot water	1L
16 oz.	uncooked cheese-filled tortellini	500 g
½ lb.	fresh asparagus, cut in 2" (5 cm) lengths	250 g
¼ cup	lemon juice	60 mL
3 tbsp.	olive oil	45 mL
2 tbsp.	water	30 mL
1 tbsp.	Worcestershire sauce	15 mL
	freshly ground pepper	
1	garlic clove, finely chopped	1
1	head romaine lettuce, torn	1
¼ cup	freshly grated Parmesan cheese	60 mL
	fresh lemon zest	

Method Bring water to full boil and cook pasta according to package directions. Drain and rinse with cold water. Steam rinsed asparagus in a covered dish on high in microwave for 4 minutes. Whisk next 6 ingredients in large bowl, until blended. Add lettuce, cheese, cooled tortellini and cooled asparagus and toss well. Top with grated Parmesan and fresh lemon zest.

Serves 6-8

Potato Caesar Salad with Prosciutto

4	slices prosciutto	4
3	slices rye bread	3
	olive oil spray	
3	unpeeled red potatoes	3
1	large head romaine lettuce, torn	1
4 tbsp.	Parmesan cheese	60 mL
2 tbsp.	capers	30 mL
	extra lettuce	

Dijon Dressing:

1 tbsp.	Dijon mustard	15 mL
2	garlic cloves, crushed	2
2 tbsp.	Parmesan cheese	30 mL
¾ cup	low-fat yogurt	175 mL
2 tbsp.	olive oil	30 mL
2 tbsp.	lemon juice	30 mL
2 tbsp.	chopped fresh basil	30 mL

Method   Grill prosciutto until crisp; break into pieces. Coat bread on both sides with oil spray. Grill on both sides and cut into cubes. Cook potatoes until tender, rinse under cold water and slice.

Blend dressing ingredients together until smooth. Combine lettuce, potatoes, bread crumbs, half the prosciutto, half the cheese in a large bowl and toss gently. Scoop into a lettuce-lined salad bowl and top with remaining prosciutto and cheese. Drizzle with dressing.

Serves   6-8

Warm Potato Brie Salad

6	unpeeled new potatoes, cooked, sliced	6
⅓ cup	olive oil	75 mL
2 tbsp.	white wine vinegar	30 mL
½ cup	sliced red onion	125 mL
½ cup	chopped fresh basil	125 mL
½ cup	chopped fresh parsley	125 mL
	salt and pepper	
4½ oz.	Brie or Camembert, cubed	130 g
	sliced radishes, basil and parsley for garnish	

Method   Combine the potatoes, oil, vinegar, onion, basil, parsley, salt and pepper. Stir in cubed cheese. Microwave on high for 30 seconds. Top with sliced radishes, fresh basil and parsley.

Serves   6-8

Goat Cheese Pasta Salad with Tomatoes and Basil

8 oz.	fusilli pasta	250 g
8 tbsp.	olive oil	125 mL
4 tbsp.	sherry vinegar	60 mL
2 tbsp.	balsamic or red wine vinegar	30 mL
¼ tsp.	dried, crushed red pepper	1 mL
¼ tsp.	salt	1 mL
4	large plum tomatoes, seeded, chopped	4
4	large green onions, thinly sliced	4
18	Kalamata olives, pitted	18
4 oz.	salami, chopped	125 g
11 oz.	soft herb goat cheese, cut into thin strips	310 g
½ cup	packed fresh basil leaves, cut into thin strips	125 mL
	salt and pepper	
	red leaf lettuce leaves	
	fresh basil leaves	

Method

Cook pasta in large pot of boiling salted water until just tender but still firm to bite, stirring occasionally. Drain. Rinse under cold water and drain well. Transfer to large bowl. Toss with 2 tbsp. (30 mL) oil. Cover and refrigerate until cold, about 2 hours.

Combine both vinegars, crushed red pepper and salt in a small bowl. Gradually whisk in the remaining 6 tbsp. oil. Pour dressing over pasta. Add tomatoes, green onions, olives and salami and toss to coat. Cover and refrigerate until ready to serve.

Just before serving, add goat cheese and sliced basil to salad and toss to combine. Season to taste with salt and pepper. Line platter with lettuce leaves. Mound salad in center. Garnish with basil leaves and serve.

Serves   4

Bacon-wrapped Scallop Salad with Pears in Pear Vinaigrette

A perfect starter – the pears and scallops are a match made in heaven!

Pear Vinaigrette:

½ cup	olive oil	125 mL
½ cup	finely chopped peeled ripe pear	125 mL
3 tbsp.	pear vinegar or white wine vinegar	45 mL
½ tbsp.	chopped fresh tarragon	7 mL
½ tsp.	sugar	2 mL
	salt and pepper	
16	bacon slices	16
16	large sea scallops, side muscle removed if necessary	16
16	¼" (1 cm) thick rounds fresh pear (about 1½" [4 cm] diameter)	16
16	fresh tarragon leaves	16
6 cups	mixed baby lettuce greens	1.5 L
⅓ cup	chopped toasted walnuts	75 mL

Method

Dressing: Purée first 5 ingredients in processor. Season dressing to taste with salt and pepper.

Lay 1 bacon slice on work surface. Place 1 scallop at end. Top scallop with pear round. Top with 1 tarragon leaf. Roll up to enclose. Cut bacon. Give wrapped scallop one-quarter turn. Place at end of bacon and roll again, completely enclosing scallop. Secure with toothpick. Repeat with remaining bacon, scallops, pears and tarragon leaves.

Heat barbecue to medium high. Grill scallop packets until bacon is crisp and scallops are cooked through, about 4 minutes per side. Divide greens among 4 plates. Top each with 4 scallops. Drizzle with dressing to moisten well. Garnish with walnuts. Pass extra dressing separately.

Serves 4

Jerk Chicken Salad in Endive Spears

Jerk Seasoning:

2 tsp.	sugar	10 mL
1 tsp.	dried thyme, crushed	5 mL
1 tsp.	ground allspice	5 mL
½ tsp.	ground black pepper	2 mL
¼ tsp.	salt	1 mL
¼ tsp.	ground red pepper	1 mL
¼ tsp.	ground nutmeg	1 mL
⅛ tsp.	ground cloves	0.5 mL
1 tbsp.	cooking oil	15 mL
1	boneless, skinless, chicken breast (3 oz.[85 g]) chopped	1
⅓ cup	finely chopped onion	75 mL
1 oz.	fully cooked ham, chopped	30 g
½ cup	chopped fresh pineapple	125 mL
1	medium tomato, seeded and finely chopped	1
¼ cup	dairy sour cream	60 mL
32	Belgian endive leaves	32

Method In a small bowl, stir together sugar, thyme, allspice, black pepper, salt, red pepper, nutmeg and cloves. Add chicken to spice mixture; toss to coat well.

Heat oil in a skillet. Add chicken and onion; stir-fry over medium-high heat until chicken is no longer pink. Do not burn. Remove from skillet. Cool chicken mixture; cover and chill.

To serve, add ham, pineapple, tomato and sour cream to chicken mixture. Toss to mix well. Separate endive leaves. Place about 1 tbsp. (15 mL) of chicken salad mixture in each leaf.

Serves 8-10

Honey Walnut Chicken Salad

Taste this to believe it! Pile it into a pineapple shell and surround with fruit drizzled with more vinaigrette.

1	whole chicken breast, cooked, boned, and skinned	1
¼	cantaloupe, peeled and seeded	¼
¼ cup	coarsely chopped walnuts	60 mL
½ cup	Dijon vinaigrette (below)	125 mL
2 tbsp.	honey	30 mL
¼	head fancy leaf lettuce, torn	¼
¼	head thinly sliced iceberg lettuce	¼
4	strawberries	4
1	slice fresh pineapple, quartered	1

Method Cool chicken and cut into thin strips. Cut cantaloupe into chunks. In bowl, combine chicken, cantaloupe and walnuts. Combine vinaigrette and honey. Pour half the vinaigrette dressing over chicken mixture and mix.

Line a large serving bowl with leaf lettuce. Put iceberg lettuce in lined bowl. Place chicken mixture in center of lettuce. Garnish with strawberries and pineapple. Serve with remaining dressing.

Serves 2-3

Dijon Vinaigrette

4 tbsp.	Dijon mustard	60 mL
3 tbsp.	red wine vinegar	45 mL
1 tbsp.	white wine vinegar	15 mL
2 tbsp.	honey	30 mL
1 tbsp.	finely chopped onion	15 mL
½	garlic clove, crushed	½
1 tsp.	chopped fresh basil	5 mL
½ tsp.	pepper	2 mL
	salt to taste	
2 drops	Tabasco sauce	2 drops
¾ cup	safflower oil	175 mL

Method Combine mustard, vinegars and honey in blender. Add onion, garlic, basil, pepper, salt and Tabasco. Blend. With machine running add oil, 1 tbsp. (15 mL) at a time. Put vinaigrette in bowl, cover and chill. Keeps several weeks.

Makes 1 cup (250 mL)

Note: The vinaigrette flavor may be varied with the use of almost any fresh herb.

Sautéed Pepper and Salami Salad

1	large red pepper	1
1	large green pepper	1
1	large yellow pepper	1
¼ cup	olive oil	60 mL
2	garlic cloves, crushed	2
½ tsp.	chopped fresh thyme	2 mL
3½ oz.	salami, sliced	100 g
1 head	mignonette lettuce	1 head
½ bunch	curly endive	½ bunch
½ cup	shredded fresh basil leaves	125 mL

Balsamic Vinegar Dressing:

4 tbsp.	olive oil	60 mL
2 tbsp.	lemon juice	30 mL
2 tbsp.	balsamic vinegar	30 mL
½ tsp.	ground black pepper	2 mL
2	garlic cloves, crushed	2

Method

Cut peppers into diamond shapes. Heat oil in a sauté pan, add peppers, garlic and thyme. Cook, stirring, 2 minutes. Cover; cook over low heat about 5 minutes, or until peppers are just tender; cool.

Cut salami into ⅕" (5 mm) strips. Combine salami, pepper mixture, lettuce, endive and basil in bowl. Just before serving, prepare dressing and toss with salad ingredients.

Dressing: Combine all dressing ingredients in a blender.

Serves

6

Vegetables
&
Side Dishes

Wild Mushroom Risotto

2	large heads garlic (about 40 cloves) cloves separated, unpeeled	2
4 tbsp.	olive oil	60 mL
¾ oz.	dried porcini mushrooms	21 g
¾ lb.	mixed fresh wild mushrooms (such as shiitake and crimini, stems trimmed from shiitake), sliced	365 g
	salt and pepper to taste	
1 cup	chopped shallots	250 mL
2 tbsp.	chopped fresh thyme or 2 tsp. (10 mL) dried	30 mL
1½ cups	arborio rice or medium-grain white rice	375 mL
½ cup	dry white wine	125 mL
3½-4 cups	chicken stock	875 mL-1 L
2 cups	thinly sliced fresh spinach leaves	500 mL
⅓ cup	freshly grated Parmesan cheese	75 mL

Method

Roasted Garlic: Preheat oven to 400°F (200°C). Combine garlic and 2 tbsp. (30 mL) oil in small baking dish. Bake, stirring occasionally, until garlic is golden and tender when pierced with small sharp knife, about 50 minutes. Cool slightly; peel garlic. Chop enough garlic to measure ¼ cup (60 mL) packed.

Place porcini in small bowl. Pour enough hot water over to cover. Let stand until soft, about 30 minutes. Drain porcini. Squeeze porcini dry and coarsely chop.

Heat 1 tbsp. (15 mL) oil in large nonstick skillet over medium-high heat. Add fresh mushrooms and sauté until golden and juices evaporate, about 7 minutes. Add porcini and stir 1 minute. Season with salt and pepper. Set aside

Heat 1 tbsp. (15 mL) oil in medium-sized, heavy saucepan over medium-high heat. Add shallots and thyme and sauté until tender, about 4 minutes. Add rice and stir to coat with shallot mixture. Add wine and cook until almost evaporated. Mix in chopped garlic and 3½ cups (875 mL) chicken stock; bring to boil. Reduce heat to medium and cook until rice is tender and mixture is creamy, about 20 minutes. Stir occasionally and add more broth if risotto is dry. Add mushroom mixture and spinach. Stir until spinach wilts. Stir in Parmesan cheese. Season to taste with salt and pepper.

Serves   8-10

Red Hot Potato Wedges

*Heat them up or tone them down by altering Tabasco sauce –
or how about trying the new green Tabasco – milder yet.*

½ cup	vegetable oil	125 mL
4	large garlic cloves, pressed	4
3 tbsp.	fresh lime juice	45 mL
2 tsp.	Tabasco sauce	10 mL
1 tsp.	chopped fresh thyme or ¼ tsp. (1 mL) dried	5 mL
	salt to taste	
6	large russet or red potatoes, each cut in 8 wedges	6

Method Whisk first 5 ingredients in small bowl to blend. Season with salt. Arrange potatoes in 9 x 13" (23 x 33 cm) glass baking dish. Season with salt. Set aside ¼ cup (60 mL) oil mixture; pour remainder over potatoes and toss to coat. Let stand for 30 minutes. Drain.

Preheat oven to 400°F (200°C). Roast potatoes until crisp and brown, turning occasionally, about 1 hour. Drizzle reserved ¼ cup (60 mL) oil mixture over potatoes.

Serves 6-8

Pink Potatoes

*These "romantic potatoes" came to me in a dream.
The perfect accompaniment to an intimate dinner.*

4	large russet potatoes, scrubbed	4
4 oz.	container smoked salmon cream cheese	125 g
1	green onion, chopped	1
¼ cup	sour cream	60 mL
dash	Tabasco sauce	dash
	freshly ground pepper	
	melted butter mixed with paprika	

Method Bake potatoes at 350°F (180°C) for 60 minutes. Cut in half and scoop out centers. While still warm, beat potato pulp until fluffy. Beat in cheese, onion, sour cream, Tabasco and pepper. Pipe filling into potato shells. Brush with butter and paprika. Bake at 350°F (180°C) for 20 minutes.

Serves 4

Potatoes Florentine

Make these ahead, cover and chill. Bake just before serving.

6	large potatoes, mashed	6
¼ cup	butter	60 mL
2	eggs	2
¼ cup	Parmesan cheese	60 mL
	salt, pepper and nutmeg to taste	
10 oz.	pkg. frozen chopped spinach	283 g
	Parmesan cheese for topping	

Method Whip potatoes, butter, eggs, cheese and spices. Fold in spinach. Bake at 350°F (180°C) for 40 minutes. Top with additional cheese.

Serves 6-8

Honey Orange Potato Swirls

Pipe these into hollowed out mini pumpkins!

3	6-8 oz. (170-250 g) white potatoes	3
3	6-8 oz.(170-250 g) yams	3
2 tsp.	milk	10 mL
4 tbsp.	butter or margarine	60 mL
2 tbsp.	orange juice	30 mL
1 tbsp.	honey	15 mL

Method Peel and quarter potatoes. In separate saucepans cook white potatoes and yams in a small amount of salted water, covered, about 20 minutes, or until potatoes are tender. Drain. In a small bowl, beat hot white potatoes with an electric mixer on low speed until almost smooth. Add milk and 2 tbsp. (30 mL) of butter. Beat until light and fluffy.

In a separate bowl, beat yams with an electric mixer at low speed until almost smooth. Add remaining butter, plus orange juice and honey. Continue beating until light and fluffy.

Line a baking sheet with foil. Spray with nonstick coating. Spoon white potato mixture into one side of a decorating bag fitted with a wide tip. Spoon yam mixture into decorating bag along side the white potatoes. For swirls, pipe 3" (7 cm) circles of the mixture onto the prepared baking sheet, starting from the outside and working toward the center, making a peak 2 layers high. Make 8 swirls. Cover loosely with plastic wrap; chill until baking time.

Bake, uncovered, in a 375°F (190°C) oven for 15-20 minutes, or until the tips are golden and swirls are heated through. Use a wide spatula to carefully transfer the swirls to dinner plates.

Serves 8

Pictured on opposite page.

Christmas Buffet

Whole Boneless Turkey with Apricot Stuffing, page 125
Honey Orange Potato Swirls, page 86
Cranberry-Kumquat Relish, page 57
Golden Baked Onions, page 94
Holiday Dinner Rolls, page 40
Brandied Orange Babas, page 174
Berry Eggnog Punch, page 190

Sweet Potato Casserole with Hazelnuts and Maple Syrup

5	medium sweet potatoes	5
½ cup	butter at room temperature	125 mL
¼ cup	brown sugar	50 mL
2	large eggs	2
½ tsp.	salt	2 mL
1 cup	milk	250 mL
2 tbsp.	maple syrup	30 mL
½ cup	chopped hazelnuts, toasted	250 mL

Method   Pierce sweet potatoes and place on paper towels in microwave oven. Microwave at high for 15-20 minutes, or until tender. When cool enough to handle, peel sweet potatoes and mash well. You should have about 3 cups (750 mL).

Place sweet potatoes, butter, sugar, eggs, salt and milk in a large bowl; beat until smooth. Place in greased 2-quart (2 L) microwaveable casserole. Microwave at medium for 3 minutes; stir. Combine maple syrup and hazelnuts and sprinkle over sweet potato mixture. Microwave at medium for 5 minutes, or until heated through.

Serves   8-10

Pecan Yam Casserole Piped into Mini Pumpkin Shells

3 cups	cooked, mashed yams	750 mL
½ cup	brown sugar	125 mL
2	eggs, beaten	2
1 cup	toasted, chopped pecans	250 mL
	salt and pepper	
	freshly ground nutmeg	
4	mini-pumpkins	4

Method   Beat yams, brown sugar and eggs until fluffy. Fold in toasted pecans and seasoning.

Bake mini pumpkins 30-45 minutes at 350°F (180°C). When softened, cut off top and scoop out pulpy interior. Pipe or mound yam mixture into shells. top with more chopped pecans and nutmeg. Bake an additional 20 minutes. Serve hot with pumpkin lids sitting lightly on top.

Serves   4

Mango Carrots with Pine Nuts

Pretty as a picture!

1 lb.	carrots, cut in thin sticks	500 g
2 tbsp.	butter	30 mL
4 tbsp.	mango purée*	60 mL
	salt and pepper	
2 tsp.	tarragon	10 mL
½ cup	toasted pine nuts	125 mL
	pine nuts and tarragon for garnish	

Method Steam carrots, with ½ cup (125 mL) of water, covered, for 5 minutes in microwave. Drain. Add remaining ingredients and microwave 1 minute longer. Top with more pine nuts and tarragon.

Serves 4

* If mango purée is unavailable, process or blend drained canned mango or fresh ripe sliced mango until smooth.

Pictured on page 121.

Lemon-Garlic Fiddleheads

Like fresh asparagus, these aren't always available – but when they are, go for it!

2 cups	fresh or frozen fiddleheads	250 mL
½ cup	butter	125 mL
2	garlic cloves, crushed	2
1	small lemon, juice of	1
	salt and pepper to taste	

Method If using fresh fiddleheads, wash and trim the ends. Steam fiddleheads for 10-12 minutes. Heat butter in pan and sauté garlic. Add fiddleheads and sauté 1 minute. Squeeze lemon juice over mixture and cook gently a further 2 minutes. Season to taste with salt and pepper.

Serves 4

Spinach and Pear Purée (La Mousseline d'Épinards aux Poires)

Very green, but oh so good! This is excellent with beef.

2½ lbs.	fresh spinach, or 3 pkgs. (10 oz. [283 g] each) frozen spinach	1.25 kg
2 tbsp.	coarse salt	30 mL
2	whole Bartlett pears or 7 oz. (213 g) can unsweetened pear, halves in syrup, drained	2
7 tbsp.	unsalted butter	105 mL
	salt to taste	
	pinch freshly grated nutmeg	

Method

If you are using fresh spinach, remove the stems and wash the spinach leaves in several changes of cold water; drain,

In a large saucepan, bring 3 quarts (3 L) of water and the coarse salt to a boil. Add the spinach and let the water return to a boil. Immediately turn the spinach into a colander and drain. Fill the saucepan with cold water and plunge the spinach into it to refresh the leaves; drain again. Squeeze handfuls of the spinach between the palms of your hands to extract all the excess water and form the spinach into compact balls. All this can be done several hours ahead and the spinach balls refrigerated until you prepare the purée.

If you are using frozen spinach, simply thaw and drain it before preparing the purée.

Drain the pears if using canned pears; if using whole pears, remove the stems and cores.

Shortly before serving, place the spinach and pears in a food processor or a food mill and reduce to a fine purée. Melt the butter in a large skillet. When the foam subsides and the butter is a light nut brown color, add the spinach and pear purée. Season with salt and grated nutmeg and stir until heated.

Serve in a warm vegetable dish.

Serves

6

Sweet Chard Tart

*A cooking class in Southern France taught me this one
– an unusual combination of savory and sweet!*

8 oz.	crème pâtissière (recipe follows)	250 mL
14 oz.	pâte sucrée (recipe follows)	400 g
20 oz.	chard/white beet leaves	600 g
3½ oz.	pine nuts	100 g
3½ oz.	raisins	100 g
1	egg	1

Method

Prepare crème pâtissière and pâte sucrée.

Wash the chard in a lot of water. Put the leaves into boiling water for 5 minutes. Take the leaves out, pass them under cold water and drain them. Refresh them one at a time and press them very well between your hands to extract as much water as possible. Chop the leaves coarsely and add them to the crème pâtissière, with the pine nuts and the raisins.

Divide the pâte sucrée into 2 equal parts. Roll out the first part to a thickness of ½2" (2 mm). Lay the dough on a large cooking sheet and cover it with the mixture of crème pâtissière, nuts and raisins, leaving a border ¼" (1 cm) wide around the edge of the dough.

Beat the egg. With a pastry brush, brush the border of the dough with the egg mixture. Cover the dough and the egg mixture with the second part of the dough that has also been rolled out to a thickness of ½2" (2 mm). Press the edges together well so that they are sealed. Leave to rest in the refrigerator for 10 minutes.

Brush the tart with the remaining egg mixture, prick with a fork and then bake at 375°F (190°C) for 20-25 minutes.

Serves 6-8

Crème Pâtissière:

3	egg yolks	3
¼ cup	sugar	60 mL
pinch	salt	pinch
¼ cup	flour or cornstarch	60 mL
1 cup	milk, heated	250 mL
2 tsp.	vanilla	10 mL
1 tbsp.	rum	15 mL

Method

Whisk the yolks and sugar until thick and creamy. Add salt and flour. Whisk well. Whisk in hot milk. Microwave on medium-high for 3 minutes. Whisk again. Microwave another 2 minutes, until thick and creamy. Stir in vanilla and rum.

Sweet Chard Tart

Continued

Pâte Sucrée (Sweet Pastry):

1 cup	flour	250 mL
¼ tsp.	salt	1 mL
½ cup	chilled unsalted butter	125 mL
1 tbsp.	water	15 mL
¼ tsp.	salt	1 mL
1	egg yolk	1
3 tbsp.	sugar	45 mL
1 tsp.	vanilla	5 mL
1 tbsp.	water	15 mL

Method   Process first 4 ingredients until crumbly. Add remaining ingredients and process on/off until mixed. Form a ball, wrap and chill. (Alternative to pâte sucrèe: Use puff pastry – it is much easier.)

Caramelized Onion Tart

This dish can be served as an appetizer, a side dish or as a light entrée.

4	bacon slices, chopped	4
3 tbsp.	butter	45 mL
4 lbs.	onions, thinly sliced	2 kg
	salt and white pepper	
½ x 17¼ oz.	box frozen puff pastry, thawed	½ x 500 g

Method   Cook bacon in large heavy skillet over medium heat until golden, about 8 minutes. Reduce heat to low and add butter and onions. Sauté until onions are brown and of a jam-like consistency, about 1 hour. Season with salt and pepper. This can be made 1 day ahead. Cover; chill. Return to room temperature before using.

Roll out pastry sheet to 13" (33 cm) square. Fit pastry into 11" (28 cm) diameter tart pan with removable bottom; trim off excess dough. Freeze 30 minutes.

Preheat oven to 425°F (220°C). Fill crust with onions. Bake until crust is golden, about 25 minutes. Cool slightly.

Serves   6

Golden Baked Onions

One of our best-ever-sellers at Candlelight Cuisine! This is incredible with a turkey dinner.

Mushroom Sauce:

2 tbsp.	butter	30 mL
½ cup	finely minced mushrooms	125 mL
2 tbsp.	flour	30 mL
1½ cups	milk or light cream	375 mL
	salt and pepper to taste	
½ cup	melted butter	125 mL
6	medium onions, sliced	6
¾ lb.	Gruyère or Swiss cheese, grated	340 g
	French bread slices	

Method   **Mushroom Sauce:** Sauté mushrooms in butter until browned. Stir in flour; whisk in milk or cream, salt and freshly ground pepper. Cook over medium heat until thick and creamy.

Preheat oven to 350°F (180°C). Butter a 2-quart (2 L) shallow oval baking dish. Melt the butter in a large skillet over medium heat. Add onions and cook until tender and translucent, stirring frequently, about 15 minutes. Transfer onions to prepared dish and set aside the remaining melted butter to use with the bread. Pour mushroom sauce over onions. Sprinkle with grated cheese. Dip bread slices in melted butter on one side. Arrange buttered side up over onion mixture to cover completely. Bake until bread is browned, about 30 minutes. Serve hot.

Serves   8-10

Pictured on page 87.

Roasted Golden Onion Flowers

6	large white onions, peeled	6
6 tbsp.	melted butter	90 mL
¼ cup	chopped pecans	60 mL
	salt and pepper to taste	

Method   Trim the root end of each onion so it will sit flat. Cut parallel vertical slices at ½" (1 cm) intervals into but not right through the onions, stopping about ½" (1.3 cm) above root end. Rotate onions 90° and cut parallel vertical slices to form a criss cross pattern. Arrange onions root end down, in a buttered shallow baking dish large enough to let onion flowers open. Drizzle with melted butter and season with salt and freshly ground pepper. Bake onions at 350°F (180°C) for about 1 hour, basting often. Sprinkle with pecans and continue baking 30 minutes longer.

Serves   6

Grilled Vegetable Antipasto Platter

For a spectacular main dish presentation, add grilled prawns – serve with foccacia.

2	eggplants	2
2 tsp.	salt	10 mL
1	EACH, sweet red and yellow pepper	1
2	zucchini	2
1	large red onion	1
12	mushrooms	12
	olive oil	
6 oz.	mozzarella or provolone cheese, thinly sliced	170 g
6 oz.	assorted Italian cold cuts (salami, prosciutto, cooked ham), thinly sliced	170 g
1	tomato, cut in wedges	1
½ cup	black olives	125 mL

Basil Balsamic Dressing:

½ cup	olive oil	125 mL
⅓ cup	chopped fresh basil	75 mL
1 tbsp.	balsamic vinegar or 2 tbsp, (30 mL) red wine vinegar	15 mL
1 tbsp.	Dijon mustard	15 mL
3	garlic cloves, minced	3
½ tsp.	each salt and pepper	2 mL

Method

Cut eggplant, into ½" (1.3 cm) thick slices. In colander, sprinkle eggplant with salt; toss to coat and let drain for 30 minutes. Place peppers on greased grill 4-6" (10-15 cm) from medium-hot coals or on medium-high setting. Grill, turning often, for 15-20 minutes, until charred. Let cool slightly. Peel, seed and cut peppers into 1" (2.5 cm) wide strips. Set aside. Diagonally cut zucchini into ½" (1.3 cm) thick slices. Cut onion into ½" (1.3 cm) thick slices. Trim stems from mushrooms. Rinse eggplant under cold water; pat dry. Lightly brush vegetables with oil. Grill mushrooms and onions for 8-10 minutes, turning occasionally, then eggplant and zucchini for 10-15 minutes, or until vegetables are tender but not charred. Set aside separately.

In a bowl, whisk together all dressing ingredients. Add mushrooms and turn to coat; transfer mushrooms to large shallow baking dish. Repeat with onion, then zucchini, peppers and eggplant, arranging vegetables separately in the dish. Refrigerate and marinate for at least 8 or up to 24 hours. Just before serving, arrange the remaining ingredients with the vegetables. Serve either at room temperature or chilled.

Serves 10

Grilled Marinated Vegetables with Lemon-Herb Marinade

Lemon-Herb Marinade:

⅔ cup	olive oil	150 mL
⅓ cup	fresh lemon juice	75 mL
⅓ cup	dry vermouth	75 mL
2 tbsp.	crumbled dried rosemary	30 mL
1 tbsp.	crumbled dried thyme	15 mL
½ tsp.	sugar	2 mL
½ tsp.	salt	2 mL
½ tsp.	pepper	2 mL
8	zucchini, halved lengthwise	8
8	crookneck squash or pattypan squash, halved lengthwise	8
4	red bell peppers, quartered lengthwise	4
8	mushrooms	8
	salt and pepper	

Method Whisk all marinade ingredients in medium bowl to blend. Makes about 1⅓ cups (325 mL). Cover and refrigerate. Bring to room temperature before using.

Arrange all vegetables in a glass baking dish. Pour marinade over. Let stand 30 minutes at room temperature.

Heat barbecue to high. Remove vegetables from marinade. Grill until golden, turning frequently with tongs, about 10 minutes. Transfer to platter. Season with salt and pepper and serve immediately.

Serves 8

Vegetable Moussaka

3	medium eggplant or 3 large zucchini	3
2 tbsp.	salt	30 mL
1½	large onions, peeled, quartered	1½
6 tbsp.	oil	90 mL
1 cup	minced parsley	250 mL
4 tbsp.	tomato paste	60 mL
⅓ cup	wine	75 mL
¾ tsp.	cinnamon	3 mL
1 tsp.	salt	5 mL
	pepper	
¼ cup	Parmesan cheese	60 mL

Ricotta Topping:

4 tbsp.	butter	60 mL
3 tbsp.	flour	45 mL
2 cups	milk	500 mL
1 tsp.	salt	5 mL
	pepper	
2	eggs	2
	fresh nutmeg	
1¼ cups	ricotta or cottage cheese	300 mL

Method Slice eggplant or zucchini ¼" (1 cm) thick. Salt the slices with the 2 tbsp. (30 mL) of salt and drain on paper towels for 30 minutes. Sauté onions in 2 tbsp. (30 mL) oil. Add parsley, tomato paste, wine, cinnamon, salt and pepper. Set aside. Sauté vegetable slices in 4 tbsp. (60 mL) oil, just steam, do not over cook. Place in buttered 9 x 12" (23 x 30 cm) casserole; sprinkle with ¼ cup (60 mL) Parmesan cheese; spread tomato mixture over this and top with rest of Parmesan cheese.

Topping: Melt butter, add flour and cook about 5 minutes. Add milk; whisk well. Cook until smooth and thick. Add salt and pepper. Cool slightly. In processor, using plastic blade, blend eggs, nutmeg and cheese, using off and on turns. Add slowly to milk mixture, stirring continually. Pour over casserole. Bake at 375°F (190°C) about 1 hour. Cool about ½ hour before serving.

Serves 6-8

Gougère au Légume

Don't be intimidated by the French title! It's a huge savory cream puff with an unbelievable filling!

Légume Filling:

1 tbsp.	butter or margarine	15 mL
1 tbsp.	flour	15 mL
½ cup	vegetable or chicken stock	125 mL
	salt and pepper	
2 tsp.	chopped fresh herbs	10 mL
2 oz.	mushrooms, sliced	55 g
4 oz.	cooked carrots, cut in julienne strips	115 g
½ cup	chopped onion	125 mL
2 tbsp.	EACH grated cheese and dry breadcrumbs mixed	30 mL

Choux Pastry:

½ cup	water	125 mL
4 tbsp.	butter or margarine	60 mL
½ cup	all-purpose flour, sifted	125 mL
pinch	EACH salt, pepper and dry mustard	pinch
2	eggs, beaten	2
½ cup	finely diced Swiss cheese	125 mL

Method

Filling: Melt the butter for the filling in a small saucepan and add the flour. Cook for 1-2 minutes, until pale straw-colored. Gradually whisk in the stock until smooth. Add a pinch of salt and pepper and the chopped herbs. Stir in the sliced mushrooms, carrots and onion and set aside.

Choux Pastry: Place the water for the pastry in a small saucepan. Cut the butter into small pieces and add to the water. Bring slowly to boil, making sure that the butter is completely melted before the water comes to a rapid boil. Turn up the heat and allow to boil rapidly for 30 seconds.

Sift the flour with a pinch of salt. Take the pan off the heat and add the flour all at once. Stir quickly and vigorously until the mixture comes away from the sides of the pan. Spread onto a plate to cool. Add salt, pepper and dry mustard to the paste and return it to the saucepan. Gradually add the egg to the paste mixture, beating well between each addition; this may be done by hand, with an electric mixer or in a food processor. It may not be necessary to add all the egg. The mixture should be smooth and shiny and hold its shape when ready. If it is still too thick, beat in the remaining egg. Stir in the diced cheese by hand.

Gougère au Légume

Continued

Spoon the paste mixture into a 10" (25 cm) deep-dish, ovenproof pie plate or 4 individual dishes, pushing the mixture slightly up the sides of the dish and leaving a well in the center. Fill the center with the filling and scatter over grated cheese and dry breadcrumbs, mixed. Bake in a preheated 400°F (200°C) oven until the pastry is puffed and brown, about 30-40 minutes. Serve immediately.

Serves Cooked in a large dish or 4 individual dishes, this makes a main course for 4 with a salad or vegetables.

Variations: This can be cooked in 6 smaller individual dishes to make a nice first course for 6.

Ham, chicken, game or shellfish can be added.

Barbecued Corn with Sun-Dried Tomato Butter

A summer sensation!

Sun-Dried Tomato Butter:

2 tbsp.	chopped parsley	30 mL
1	garlic clove	1
2 tbsp.	chopped chives	30 mL
4 tbsp.	chopped sun-dried tomatoes	60 mL
¾ cup	softened butter or margarine	175 mL
2 tsp.	lemon juice	10 mL
	Tabasco sauce to taste	
8	ears of corn	8

Method In processor chop parsley, garlic, chives and tomatoes. Add butter and lemon juice. Season with Tabasco. Make this ahead so flavors marry.

Peel back corn husks, discard silk. Spread each ear of corn with about 1 tbsp. (15 mL) tomato butter. Replace husks and carefully wrap in foil. This can be done hours ahead and the ears chilled.

Roast corn on barbecue about 30 minutes, turning often. Unwrap corn and brush with more tomato butter.

Serves 6-8

Asparagus Soufflé

This dramatic and beautiful presentation does justice to the incomparable flavor of fresh asparagus.

2 lbs.	asparagus	1 kg
	vegetable-oil spray	
1 tbsp.	butter or margarine	15 mL
1 tbsp.	vegetable oil	15 mL
3 tbsp.	snipped fresh chives	45 mL
3 tbsp.	flour	45 mL
1 cup	skim or low-fat milk	250 mL
1	egg yolk, lightly beaten	1
½ tsp.	salt (optional)	2 mL
	freshly ground black pepper to taste	
3	egg whites	3
½ tsp.	cream of tartar	2 mL

Method

Cut the asparagus tips into lengths equal to the depth of a 1-quart (1 L) soufflé dish plus ½" (1.3 cm). If there are not enough tips to completely line the dish, cut some of the remaining stems to the same length. Remove the asparagus pieces from the dish, and set them aside.

Dice enough of the remaining asparagus to make 1 cup (250 mL) of pieces. Steam the pieces for 5 minutes, and purée them in a food mill or food processor. Set the asparagus purée aside.

Preheat the oven to 350°F (180°C). Spray the soufflé dish with vegetable oil.

In a large saucepan, heat the butter and oil, add the chives and flour, and sauté for 1 minute. Gradually add the milk, stirring the mixture constantly to form a smooth liquid. When the mixture thickens slightly, stir in the reserved puréed asparagus, egg yolk, salt (if desired) and pepper.

In a mixing bowl, beat the egg whites on high speed until they are foamy. Add the cream of tartar, and continue beating the egg whites until they form stiff peaks. Blend ⅓ of the beaten egg whites into the asparagus mixture. Then carefully fold in the remaining ⅔ of the egg whites just until the white streaks disappear. Do not overmix the soufflé.

Pour the mixture into the prepared soufflé dish. Quickly stand the reserved asparagus spears, tips pointing up, around the edge of the dish to form a fence. Put the soufflé in the hot oven, and bake it for 40 minutes, or until the top is puffy and golden brown. Serve the soufflé immediately.

Serves

4-6

Pastas

Homemade Pasta Processor Style

So easy, so versatile! Add your own flavorings.

3 cups	flour	750 mL
2 tsp.	salt	10 mL
3	eggs	3
3 tbsp.	olive oil	45 mL
	water	

Method Process flour, salt and eggs until blended. With processor running, slowly add olive oil and just enough water to form a dough. Process to knead. When dough is smooth and satiny, let sit under a large bowl for 15 minutes. Proceed with pasta machine to form desired shapes.

Makes about 1 lb. (500 g) of pasta

Variations To flavor pasta, add with the first step 2 tbsp. (30 mL) sweet red pepper paste or pesto sauce or tomato paste.

Wine Pasta

Beautiful tender pasta!

3½ cups	flour	875 mL
1 tsp.	salt	5 mL
2	large eggs	2
¾ cup	white wine (approx.)	175 mL

Method In food processor, mix flour, salt and eggs. Slowly add wine to make firm dough. Wrap in plastic and let rest ½ hour. Proceed with pasta machine to make desired shapes.

Makes about 1 lb. (500 g) of pasta

Fresh Orange Peppered Pasta

Pasta color intensifies when it is cooked.

2 cups	flour	500 mL
2 tsp.	salt	10 mL
2	eggs	2
2 tbsp.	olive oil	30 mL
1	large red pepper, roasted and peeled	1
1 tbsp.	tomato paste	15 mL

Method Process flour, salt and eggs. Add oil, red pepper and tomato paste. Process until smooth dough is formed. If dough is dry, add just enough water until ball forms. Process until smooth and satiny. Proceed with pasta machine to make desired shape.

Makes about 1 lb. (500 g) of pasta

Tri-Colored Pasta with Sun-Dried Tomato Pesto

Sun-Dried Tomato Pesto:

1 cup	drained oil-packed sun-dried tomatoes (about 6 oz. [170 g])	250 mL
½ cup	grated Romano or Parmesan	125 mL
¼ cup	chopped fresh basil	60 mL
2 tbsp.	pine nuts, toasted	30 mL
3	garlic cloves	3
¾ cup	olive oil	175 mL
¾ lb.	Tri-Colored Pasta (recipe follows)	365 g
1 lb.	boneless chicken breasts, grilled	500 g
½ lb.	cooked prawns	250 g
	salt, pepper and Parmesan cheese	

Method **Pesto:** Combine sun-dried tomatoes, Romano cheese, basil, pine nuts and garlic in food processor. With machine running, gradually add olive oil and process until a smooth pesto paste forms. Cover and refrigerate.

Cook pasta until just tender. Drain, reserving ½ cup (125 mL) cooking liquid. Combine ¾ cup (175 mL) tomato pesto with reserved cooking liquid in pasta pot. Add pasta, chicken and prawns and toss over medium-high heat to coat, add more pesto, if desired. Season to taste with salt and pepper. Serve with additional Parmesan cheese.

Serves 6-8

Homemade Tri-Colored Pasta

Yellow Peppered Pasta:

2 cups	flour	500 mL
2 tsp.	salt	10 mL
2	eggs	2
2 tbsp.	olive oil	30 mL
1	large yellow pepper, roasted, peeled and sliced	1
1 tbsp.	saffron or turmeric	15 mL

Method Process flour, salt and eggs. Add oil, pepper and saffron. If still dry add just enough water until a smooth dough is formed. Knead until satiny. Proceed with pasta machine to make desired shapes.

Makes about 1 lb. (500 g) of pasta

Variations **Orange Peppered Pasta:** Follow recipe above substituting ½ tin of canned red pepper for yellow pepper and omitting saffron.

Spinach Pasta: See page 108.

Lemon-Peppered & Spinach Fettuccine with Sun-Dried Tomatoes & Italian Bacon

Lemon-Peppered Pasta:

3 cups	flour	750 mL
1 tsp.	salt	5 mL
1 tbsp.	cracked black pepper	15 mL
2 tbsp.	lemon zest	30 mL
3	eggs	3
2 tbsp.	olive oil	30 mL

Spinach Pasta:

3 cups	flour	750 mL
1 tsp.	salt	5 mL
2 cups	fresh spinach	500 mL
2	eggs	2
2 tbsp.	olive oil	30 mL

Creamy Sun-Dried Tomato and Bacon Sauce:

1 tbsp.	olive oil	15 mL
4	slices Italian bacon (pancetta), chopped	4
2	large shallots, chopped	2
½ cup	heavy cream	125 mL
¼ cup	sun-dried tomatoes, diced	60 mL
	salt and freshly ground pepper	
2 tbsp.	pine nuts, toasted	30 mL
	chopped, fresh parsley	
¼ cup	freshly grated Parmesan cheese	60 mL

Method

Pastas: To make EACH pasta, in food processor, mix all ingredients except eggs and oil. With machine running add eggs and oil. Process only until dough forms a ball. If dough appears dry, add a small amount of water. Proceed according to pasta machine instructions, making both fettuccines.

Sauce: To make sauce, heat oil in a heavy skillet. Add bacon and cook until crisp. Drain well. Chop bacon. Add shallots and stir 1 minute. Add cream and bring to a soft boil. Add sun-dried tomatoes and turn off heat.

Meanwhile, cook both fresh pastas in a large pot of boiling salted water until just tender, 3-4 minutes. Drain well and toss with sauce. Season with salt and pepper and top with pine nuts and parsley. Pass additional Parmesan cheese.

Serves 6-8

Tortellini of Artichokes and Mascarpone

Mascarpone cheese is a buttery, creamy cheese but if it is unavailable use cream cheese with 2 tbsp. (30 mL) sour cream added.

1	recipe of wine pasta, see page 94	1

Artichoke and Mascarpone Filling:

2	large garlic cloves, minced	2
6 tbsp.	minced onion	90 mL
1 tbsp.	EACH butter and olive oil	15 mL
14 oz.	tin artichoke hearts or bottoms, chopped	398 mL
3 tbsp.	minced fresh basil	45 mL
1	large lemon, zest and juice of	1
8 oz.	mascarpone cheese	250 g
½ cup	grated Parmesan cheese	125 mL
	freshly ground pepper	

Creamy Lemon Sauce:

1 cup	chicken stock	250 mL
4 tbsp.	butter	60 mL
4 tbsp.	mascarpone cheese	60 mL
½ cup	light cream	125 mL
1	lemon, zest and juice of	1
	pepper	
	freshly grated Parmesan cheese	
	freshly ground pepper	
	lemon zest	

Method Prepare pasta and make into wide strips.

Filling: Sauté garlic and onion in butter and oil. Add artichokes. Sauté 5-10 minutes. Add basil, lemon zest and juice. Remove from heat. Process until finely chopped. Add cheeses and pepper. Set aside.

Sauce: To make sauce, in the same pan as used for the filling, reduce chicken stock to ½ cup (125 mL). Whisk in butter 1 tbsp. (15 mL) at a time. Turn heat to low and whisk in cheese, then cream. Season with lemon zest, juice and pepper.

To assemble, cut pasta strips into large squares. Place ample amount of filling in center. Fold over diagonally and pinch seams well. Take ends and twist together. Place on towel-lined pan. Chill thoroughly. Bring large pot of water to full boil. Add tortellini in batches. Cook about 4 minutes. They will rise to the top. Lift out and drain as they rise. Ladle sauce onto plate. Top with tortellini and nap with more sauce. Top with Parmesan cheese, freshly ground pepper and more lemon zest.

Serves 6-8

Spinach Ravioli with Basil Cream Sauce

Spinach Pasta:

½ lb.	fresh spinach leaves	250 g
1½ cups	(or more) all-purpose flour	375 mL
2	eggs	2
2 tbsp.	olive oil	30 mL
	salt	

Ricotta Filling:

1 cup	ricotta cheese	250 mL
½ cup	grated Parmesan cheese	125 mL
1	egg, lightly beaten	1
2 tbsp.	minced fresh parsley	30 mL
	pinch of ground allspice	
	salt and pepper	

Basil Cream Sauce:

4 cups	whipping cream	1 L
¼ cup	unsalted butter, cut into pieces	60 mL
¼ cup	minced fresh basil	60 mL
2	small garlic cloves, minced	2
	salt and pepper to taste	
	grated Parmesan cheese	

Method

Pasta: Cook spinach in large pot of boiling water until just wilted. Drain well; squeeze dry. Mince spinach.

Mound 1½ cups (375 mL) flour on work surface or in large bowl and make well in center. Add spinach, eggs, oil and pinch of salt to well and blend with fork. Gradually draw flour from edge of well into center until all flour is incorporated. Knead dough on lightly floured surface until smooth, about 7 minutes, kneading in additional flour if sticky. Wrap in plastic and let rest 1 hour.

Cut dough into 4 pieces. Flatten 1 piece of dough (keep remainder covered), then fold in thirds. Turn pasta machine to widest setting and run dough through several times until smooth and velvety. Number of times will depend on how vigorously dough was kneaded by hand, folding before each run and dusting with flour if sticky. Adjust machine to next narrower setting. Run dough through machine without folding. Repeat, narrowing rollers after each run until pasta is ¹⁄₁₆-⅛" (0.25-0.5 cm) thick, dusting with flour as necessary. Trim edges of pasta to make a 4" (10 cm) wide sheet.

Spinach Ravioli with Basil Cream Sauce

Continued

Filling: Combine filling ingredients. Place by teaspoonfuls down length of pasta sheet, 1" (2.5 cm) in from 1 long side and 1½" (4 cm) apart. Fold pasta lengthwise in half over filling; press firmly around filling to seal. Cut pasta between filling into rectangles using large knife or pastry wheel. Arrange ravioli in single layer on lightly floured tea towel-lined baking sheet. Repeat with remaining dough and filling. (Ravioli may be frozen on cookie sheets now and put in freezer bags for storage.)

Sauce: Boil cream in heavy skillet until reduced to 2 cups (500 mL). Reduce heat. Whisk in butter, basil and garlic: add salt and pepper.

Meanwhile, add ravioli in batches to a large pot of boiling salted water. Cook until just tender but still firm to the bite, stirring to prevent sticking, 3-5 minutes for fresh (8-10 minutes for frozen). Drain ravioli well.

Add ravioli to sauce and cook over low heat until sauce thickens slightly, about 3 minutes. Divide ravioli and sauce among plates. Season with pepper. Serve, passing grated Parmesan cheese separately.

Serves 6

Carbonara

4 slices	bacon or pancetta (Italian bacon)	4
⅓ cup	cream	75 mL
pinch	paprika	pinch
1	egg	1
1	egg yolk, extra	1
2 oz.	grated Parmesan cheese	55 g
½ lb.	pkg. fettuccine or tagliatelle noodles	250 g
1 oz.	softened butter	30 g
	pepper	

Method Remove rind from bacon; cut bacon into thin strips. Cook in frying pan until crisp. Drain off fat, leaving approximately 2 tbsp. (30 mL) bacon fat. Stir in cream and paprika. Place egg, egg yolk and 1 oz. (30 g) grated Parmesan cheese into bowl; beat until combined. Cook fettuccine in boiling salted water. Boil, uncovered, 10-12 minutes, until just cooked. Drain. Return to pan with butter, toss over low heat until combined. Add bacon-cream mixture; toss until combined. Add egg mixture; toss until combined. Season with pepper. Sprinkle with remaining grated Parmesan cheese.

Serves 4-6

Peppered Ravioli Stuffed with Scallops in Smoked Salmon Cream

1	recipe homemade Fresh Peppered Pasta (below) or 1 lb. (500 g) pkg. fresh lasagne noodles	1
4 oz.	smoked salmon	125 g
8 oz.	cream cheese	250 g
2 tbsp.	chopped chives	30 mL
1 tbsp.	lime juice	15 mL
16	large scallops	16
	light cream	
	fresh dill	
1 tbsp.	grated lemon rind	15 mL
1 tbsp.	butter	15 mL
	smoked salmon rosettes	
	fresh dill, lemon wedges for garnish	

Method Roll out fresh pasta, see page 106, or lay out fresh lasagne noodles. In food processor, blend next 4 ingredients, reserving a few strips of smoked salmon. Place 1 tbsp (15 mL) of salmon mixture every 2" (5 cm), going down the strip of pasta. Place 1 scallop and a piece of salmon on each spoonful of filling. Fold pasta lengthwise over filling, pressing down around scallops to seal. Cut into ravioli squares. Chill.

Smoked Salmon Cream: Heat remaining salmon cream over low heat, thinning with light cream. Add fresh dill and grated lemon rind.

Bring a large pot of water to a full boil and add ravioli. Cook until they rise to the surface, about 3-5 minutes. Drain and toss with 1 tbsp. (15 mL) butter. Arrange on serving platter and spoon sauce over top. Decorate with smoked salmon rosettes, fresh dill and lemon wedges.

Serves 2-4

Fresh Peppered Pasta

2 cups	flour	500 mL
1 tsp.	salt	5 mL
1	red pepper, charred and peeled	1
1 tsp.	red pepper flakes	5 mL
2	egg whites	2
2 tbsp.	oil	30 mL

Method In food processor, process first 4 ingredients. Slowly add egg whites and oil, processing until smooth, satiny dough forms. If dry, add a little water. Run dough through pasta maker as for lasagne.

Makes about 1 lb. (500 g) of pasta

Pesto

2 cups	tightly packed fresh basil leaves	500 mL
2 tbsp.	pine nuts or broken walnuts	30 mL
2	large garlic cloves	2
¼ tsp.	salt, or more, to taste	1 mL
½ cup	fruity olive oil	125 mL
½ cup	freshly grated Parmesan cheese	125 mL
2 tbsp.	freshly grated Romano cheese	30 mL
	freshly ground pepper	

Method Place the basil, pine nuts, garlic and salt in food processor or blender or use a mortar and pestle. Process or pound until finely chopped or puréed. Slowly add the olive oil and continue to process until the mixture is smooth and uniform. Stir in the cheeses and freshly ground pepper.

Freezing If freezing, omit the cheeses. Stir in the cheese and correct seasonings when thawed.

Makes enough pesto for 1 lb. (500 g) of pasta.

Lemon Linguine with Garlic, Clams and Mussels

This is a wonderfully light main course – a seafood lovers' dream. Scallops and prawns may be added or substituted.

¼ cup	olive oil	60 mL
¼ cup	finely chopped shallots	60 mL
3	large garlic cloves, finely minced	3
1	orange pepper, chopped	1
2	large tomatoes, diced	2
2 lbs.	fresh clams	1 kg
2 lbs.	fresh mussels	1 kg
1 cup	dry white wine	250 mL
1 lb.	lemon linguine (or your choice)	500 g
1 cup	chopped fresh parsley	250 mL
	freshly grated Parmesan cheese	
1 tbsp.	fresh lemon zest	30 mL
	freshly ground pepper	

Method Heat oil in large heavy skillet with a lid. Add shallots and garlic and sauté just until tender. Add tomatoes, clams, mussels and wine. Cover and simmer about 10 minutes. Meanwhile, cook linguine in large pot of boiling salted water just until tender. Drain and keep warm. Toss with clam and mussel mixture and half of parsley. Serve on large platter and top with fresh Parmesan cheese, remaining parsley, lemon zest and pepper.

Serves 4-6

Seafood Lasagne

Top with giant shrimp and scallops!

Seafood Sauce:

½ cup	flour	125 mL
½ cup	butter	125 mL
2 cups	half-and-half or milk	500 mL
	salt and pepper	
2 tsp.	basil	10 mL
1 tsp.	dill	5 mL
2 tsp.	saffron threads	10 mL
½ cup	white wine	125 mL
½ cup	Swiss cheese	125 mL
¾ lb.	shrimp	365 g
½ lb.	crab or shredded crab sticks	250 g
½ lb.	scallops	250 g
4	sheets lasagne noodles (fresh preferable)	4
16 oz.	creamed cottage cheese	500 g
2 cups	shredded mozzarella cheese	500 mL
1 cup	ricotta cheese	250 mL
2 cups	shredded Swiss cheese	500 mL
	Parmesan cheese	
	chopped parsley	

Method

Sauce: Melt the butter and mix in the flour. Stir over heat, then slowly stir in the milk and cook until thickened. Add the remaining sauce ingredients and mix well. Set aside.

Butter lasagne pan. Layer in the pan; 1 sheet of lasagne; the cottage cheese; ¼ of the sauce mixture. Another sheet of lasagne; mozzarella cheese; ¼ of the sauce mixture. Another sheet of lasagne; ricotta cheese; ¼ of the sauce. Remaining lasagne sheet; Swiss cheese; remainder of the sauce. Sprinkle Parmesan cheese over top. Bake in 350°F (180°C) oven for 1 hour. Decorate top of prepared dish with chopped parsley.

Serves

8-10

Anniversary Rotolo with Chicken and Scallops

I created this divine dish at our anniversary, when Terry wanted chicken, I wanted seafood, and we both wanted pasta. Fresh Orange Peppered Pasta, page 102, makes this very colorful.

Chicken and Scallop Filling:

2 cups	cubed boneless chicken breast	500 mL
¼ cup	butter	60 mL
2	garlic cloves	2
½ lb.	large scallops	250 g
1 tbsp.	tarragon	15 mL
	salt and pepper to taste	
1 cup	heavy cream	250 mL
1 tbsp.	tomato paste	15 mL

Vegetable Filling:

2 cups	sliced mushrooms	500 mL
¼ cup	diced shallots	60 mL
2 tbsp.	butter	30 mL
½ cup	chopped, sun-dried tomatoes	125 mL

White Sauce:

2 tbsp.	butter	30 mL
2 tbsp.	flour	30 mL
1½ cups	milk	375 mL
	salt and pepper to taste	
1 tbsp.	tomato paste	15 mL
2	large sheets fresh pasta	2
1½ cups	ricotta cheese	375 mL
1 cup	Parmesan cheese	250 mL
	freshly ground pepper	
	Parmesan cheese, paprika	

Method

Chicken Filling: Sauté chicken with butter and garlic in a large skillet until almost cooked. Add scallops and seasonings. Simmer 5 minutes. Stir in cream and tomato paste and stir until thickened. Set aside.

Vegetable Filling: Sauté mushrooms and shallots in butter. Add tomatoes.

White Sauce: Melt butter, stir in flour. Add milk, seasonings and tomato paste. Microwave on medium-high, 3 minutes, or until thick. Set aside.

Lay sheets of pasta side by side. Moisten edges so they stick together. Spread softened ricotta cheese over pasta. Sprinkle with vegetable filling. Spoon chicken filling over this. Sprinkle with 1 cup (250 mL) Parmesan cheese and pepper. Roll up carefully. Transfer to greased cookie sheet. Frost rotolo roll with thick layer of white sauce. Sprinkle with Parmesan cheese and paprika. Bake at 350°F (180°C) for 25 minutes.

Serves 2-4

Stuffed Rotolo

*This may seem complicated, but do it well ahead in stages.
It is well worth it. Terry loves it cold!*

1-2	large sheets fresh pasta	1-2
	Parmesan cheese	
	butter	
	paprika	

Spinach Mixture:

2 lbs.	fresh spinach (3 heads)	1 kg
1 cup	water	250 mL
1 tbsp.	salt	15 mL
3 tbsp.	butter	45 mL
1/3 cup	Parmesan cheese	75 mL
1/4 cup	heavy cream	60 mL
	salt and freshly ground pepper to taste	

Sausage and Veal Sauce:

3 tbsp.	butter	45 mL
5-6 oz.	Italian sausage, skinned	140-170 g
6 oz.	ground veal or extra lean beef	170 g
4 oz.	sliced mushrooms	125 g
1/2 cup	water	125 mL
1 tbsp.	tomato paste	15 mL
1/4 cup	whipped cream	60 mL
	salt and pepper	

Balsamella (White Sauce):

1/4 cup	butter	60 mL
3 tbsp.	flour	45 mL
2 cups	milk	500 mL
	salt, pepper, pinch of nutmeg	

Method

Pasta: Have pasta ready to use.

Spinach Mixture: Combine washed spinach, water and salt. Cover and simmer about 3 minutes. Drain and squeeze dry. Melt butter in skillet, add spinach, Parmesan cheese and cream. Sauté 2-3 minutes. Transfer to food processor and chop coarsely.

Meat Sauce: Melt butter in large skillet; add crumbled sausage and ground veal. Cook until no longer pink. Add mushrooms, water, tomato paste, cream, salt and pepper. Cook until thick, 10-15 minutes.

Balsamella: Melt butter in small pan. Stir in flour. Whisk in milk and seasonings. Bring to a boil, whisking constantly until thickened.

Stuffed Rotolo
Continued

Stir ½ cup (125 mL) white sauce into meat sauce. Set oven to 400°F (200°C). Lay pasta sheet flat on counter. Spread meat mixture over pasta, leaving 2" (5 cm) border. Spread spinach mixture over meat mixture. Sprinkle with 3 tbsp. (45 mL) Parmesan cheese. Roll up like a jelly roll. Place on a cookie sheet. Sprinkle with Parmesan cheese, dot with butter. Bake until cheese is melted and golden, about 10-15 minutes. Remove from oven. Sprinkle with paprika. Cool 10 minutes; slice.

Serves 4-6

Pumpkin Gnocchi with Walnut Sauce

I hollowed out a big baked squash – polished it up with olive oil and piled in the gnocchi. What a fabulous presentation!

10 oz.	russet potato, peeled, quartered	285 g
1 cup	canned solid-pack pumpkin	250 mL
1½ tsp.	salt	7 mL
⅛ tsp.	ground black pepper	0.5 mL
1/8 tsp.	ground nutmeg	0.5 mL
1¼ cups	(or more) all-purpose flour	300 mL

Walnut Sauce:

2 cups	whipping cream	500 mL
¾ cup	chopped walnuts	175 mL
1 tsp.	nutmeg	5 mL
	salt and pepper, to taste	

½ cup	freshly grated Parmesan cheese	125 mL
¼ cup	fresh parsley	60 mL

Method **Pumpkin Gnocchi:** Cook potato until tender. Drain and mash. Add pumpkin, salt, pepper and nutmeg. Stir on medium heat until dry, about 5 minutes, then remove. Mix in flour to form smooth but slightly sticky dough. Knead on floured surface for about 2 minutes. Roll dough to ½" (1.3 cm) thick. Cut into strips 1" (2.5 cm) wide. Hand roll strips into long rope. Cut into pieces 1¼" (3 cm) long. Cook gnocchi, in batches, in a large pot of boiling salted water until they rise, about 2½ minutes. Drain in colander. Let stand at room temperature on a foil-lined baking sheet.

Walnut Sauce: Combine cream, walnuts and nutmeg in heavy skillet. Boil until thickened, about 6 minutes. Season with salt and pepper.

Add gnocchi to warm sauce over medium heat until heated through, about 2 minutes. Transfer to plates. Sprinkle with Parmesan and parsley.

Serves 6-8

Herbed White Asparagus Lasagne

Creamy Garlic Herb Sauce:

2 tbsp.	butter	30 mL
1	medium onion, finely chopped	1
2	garlic cloves, minced	2
¾ cup	skim milk	175 mL
10 oz.	tofu or 8 oz. (250 g) light cream cheese	285 g
½ tsp.	salt	2 mL
1 tbsp.	fresh basil	15 mL
¼ cup	grated Parmesan cheese	60 mL
½ tsp.	dry mustard	2 mL
½ tsp.	paprika	2 mL
1 tbsp.	tomato paste	15 mL
1 tbsp.	fresh dillweed	15 mL
2 cups	sliced mushrooms	500 mL
1 tbsp.	olive oil	15 mL
2 cups	prepared tomato sauce	500 mL
6-9	ready-bake or fresh lasagne sheets	6-9
½ cup	ricotta cheese	125 mL
¾ lb.	asparagus or 2, 10 oz. (284 mL) cans white asparagus	365 g
1 cup	grated soy cheese	250 mL
½ cup	sun-dried tomatoes, chopped	125 mL
½ cup	Parmesan cheese	125 mL
	paprika and herbs of choice	

Method

Sauce: Over low heat, melt butter and sauté onion and garlic. Combine with remaining sauce ingredients in processor or blender until smooth. Transfer to glass bowl and microwave about 3 minutes on medium-high. Adjust seasoning.

Sauté mushrooms in olive oil. Spray a lasagne dish. Spread ½ cup (125 mL) cream sauce on bottom of dish. Top with ½ cup (125 mL) tomato sauce. Add 1 layer lasagne noodles. Spread with the ricotta cheese and asparagus (save some for garnish). Top with ½ cup (125 mL) tomato sauce and some grated soy cheese. Add another layer of lasagne, top with half the remaining soy cheese and tomato sauce. Finish with lasagne, remaining cream sauce, soy cheese and Parmesan cheese. Sprinkle with paprika and herbs. Bake at 350°F (180°C) for 1 hour.

Serves

6-8

Main
Courses

Boneless Chicken Florentine

Spinach Filling:

1 cup	cottage cheese	250 mL
1 cup	feta cheese	250 mL
2	eggs	2
1 tbsp.	dillweed	15 mL
3 cups	washed spinach	750 mL
4	single, boneless chicken breasts	4
4	slices bacon	4
	paprika	

Method To make spinach filling, process cheeses, eggs and dill. Add spinach, processing on and off until blended. Pound chicken until smooth and even. Spread with spinach filling. Roll up. Wrap with bacon. Sprinkle with paprika. Bake at 350°F (180°C) for 1 hour.

Serves 4

Breast of Chicken Medallions with Brandied Apples and Pink Peppercorns

This is light – but oh so decadent!

4 tbsp.	chicken stock	60 mL
4	single, boneless chicken breasts	4
	salt and pepper	
	flour	
3	Granny Smith apples, sliced	3
½ cup	apple cider or Calvados	125 mL
¼ cup	brandy	60 mL
2 tbsp.	pink peppercorns	30 mL
½ cup	diced purple onion	125 mL
13½ oz.	evaporated skim milk	385 mL
2 tbsp.	flour, dissolved in milk	30 mL

Method Heat stock in large skillet. Season chicken with salt and pepper and dredge in flour. Add chicken to skillet and cook until browned on both sides, about 4 minutes. Add apple slices, both brandies, peppercorns and diced onions. Simmer over medium heat until apples are tender, about 7 minutes. Remove chicken and apples with slotted spoon and keep warm. Add milk to pan; simmer until thickened, adding flour if needed. Season with salt and pepper. Return chicken and apples to sauce and heat through. Arrange chicken on platter, spoon apples and brandy sauce over.

Serves 4

Grilled Chicken with Raspberry Ketchup

4	single, boneless chicken breasts	4
	olive oil	
	Raspberry Ketchup (below)	

Method Brush the chicken lightly with oil. Place the chicken on the grill, skin side down, and close the cover. Cook the chicken, turning frequently with tongs, until almost cooked through, about 40 minutes for dark meat and 30 minutes for white meat. All timing will depend on the heat of the fire.

Baste the meat with the Raspberry Ketchup and cook for an additional 5-10 minutes on each side, until the meat is glazed but not charred. Serve immediately with additional Raspberry Ketchup as a condiment.

Serves 2-4

Raspberry Ketchup

This superb ketchup is also perfect with pork. A great gift idea!

1 qt.	raspberries	1 L
½ cup	firmly packed light brown sugar	125 mL
2 tbsp.	water	30 mL
2	medium onions, finely chopped	2
1	large garlic clove, finely chopped	1
½ cup	white wine vinegar	125 mL
1 tbsp.	ground ginger	15 mL
½ tsp.	ground cinnamon	2 mL
½ tsp.	ground cloves	2 mL
⅛ tsp.	cayenne pepper	0.5 mL

Method Place the raspberries in a small, heavy saucepan with half the brown sugar and the water. Place over medium heat and cook, stirring occasionally and mashing the berries against the side of the pan, until the mixture comes to a boil. Reduce the heat and simmer for 5 minutes.

Remove from the heat and strain the raspberry mixture through a fine sieve to remove the seeds. Return the strained berry mixture to the pan and place over medium heat. Stir in remaining sugar and all other remaining ingredients and bring to a simmer. Reduce the heat and simmer, stirring occasionally, until the onions are very tender and the mixture has thickened.

Transfer the raspberry mixture to a food processor. Process to a smooth purée. Spoon the ketchup into sterilized 1 cup (250 mL) jars, cover tightly and refrigerate. Keeps, refrigerated, for 2 weeks.

Makes 6, 1 cup (250 mL) jars

Breast of Chicken Dijon in Flaky Phyllo Pastry

The wonder of this recipe is how beautifully it freezes prior to baking.

⅓ cup	butter	75 mL
6	single, boneless, chicken breasts cut into strips	6
¼ cup	brandy (optional)	60 mL
½ cup	Dijon mustard	125 mL
1 cup	heavy cream	250 mL
	salt and pepper	
8	sheets phyllo pastry	8
	melted butter	
	dry bread crumbs	
	paprika	

Method   Melt butter in large skillet. Sauté chicken until white. Remove from pan and set aside. Meanwhile, if using, add brandy to skillet and stir, to deglaze pan. Add mustard and cream, whisking well. Season with salt and pepper and simmer 5 minutes. Stir in chicken and simmer until hot.

Prepare phyllo pastry. Take 1 sheet and brush it with melted butter. Top with crumbs, then another phyllo sheet. Repeat layering using all 8 sheets of phyllo. Brush top layer with sauce from pan. Place chicken along short side of pastry. Spoon sauce over top and roll up like a jelly roll, tucking in sides as you roll. Brush with melted butter and sprinkle with paprika. Bake at 375°F (190°C) about 30 minutes.

Serves   6

Boneless Chicken and Seafood

½ lb.	scallops	250 g
2 tbsp.	butter	30 mL
½ lb.	crab or crab sticks	250 g
½ lb.	shrimp	250 g
4	single, boneless chicken breasts	4
	Parmesan cheese	
	salt and pepper	
	slices bacon	
	paprika	

Method   Sauté scallops in butter about 3 minutes. Add crab and shrimp. Place seafood in center of chicken breasts. Wrap breasts around filling. Sprinkle with Parmesan cheese, salt and pepper to taste. Wrap bacon around breasts. Sprinkle with cheese, salt, pepper and paprika. Bake at 350°F (180°C) for 50 minutes.

Serves   4

Boneless Grilled Chicken with Butterflied Prawns and Peppercorn Sauce

Herbed Lemon Marinade:

1 cup	olive oil	250 mL
⅓ cup	lemon juice	70 mL
3 tbsp.	dried basil	45 mL
2 tbsp.	dried oregano	30 mL
1 tbsp.	minced garlic	15 mL
1 tbsp.	hot sauce	15 mL
4	single, boneless chicken breasts	4
1 lb.	butterflied prawns	500 g

Peppercorn Sauce*:

1 tbsp.	sweet butter	15 mL
3	shallots, finely chopped	3
2 tbsp.	brandy	30 mL
1 tsp.	Dijon mustard	5 mL
½ tsp.	black peppercorns, lightly crushed	2 mL
½ tsp.	each drained, whole green and pink peppercorns	2 mL
½ cup	heavy or whipping cream	125 mL
	salt	

Method Combine all ingredients for the marinade, then add the chicken breasts and let sit overnight. Grill chicken breasts on barbecue or broil on medium-low about 10 minutes. Cover and keep warm. Prepare Peppercorn Sauce. Place chicken in pan. Top with prawns. Spoon pepper sauce over and bake about 10 minutes at 375°F (190°C).

Peppercorn Sauce: In a small skillet, heat butter. Add shallots and sauté 4 minutes, until softened. Add brandy and flame. Stir in mustard, peppercorns and cream. Bring to a boil. Reduce heat and simmer, stirring 4-5 minutes, until thickened. Taste and season with salt.

Serves 4

Pictured on front cover.

*Green Peppercorn Sauce: Use 1½ tsp. (7 mL) of green peppercorns in total, instead of using the black and pink peppercorns.

Prawns and Chicken in Pernod with Almond Chive Rice

Sounds rich – but it is surprisingly light! Check the cream!

2 tbsp.	olive oil	30 mL
1	onion, minced	1
1	fennel bulb, sliced	1
2	garlic cloves, minced	2
4	single, boneless chicken breasts, sliced	4
28 oz.	can tomatoes	796 mL
¼ cup	Pernod or sambuca	60 mL
2 tbsp.	flour	30 mL
1 cup	evaporated skim milk	250 mL
1 lb.	jumbo prawns	500 g
	salt and freshly ground pepper to taste	
2 tbsp.	pink peppercorns	30 mL

Method Heat oil in large heavy skillet. Add onion, fennel and garlic, cooking about 5 minutes. Add chicken at this point, sautéing until golden. Add tomatoes and Pernod and simmer about 10 minutes. Dissolve flour in some of the milk and stir into tomato mixture. Add the prawns and the rest of the milk, cooking about 3 minutes. Season with salt and pepper and stir in peppercorns. Spoon Prawns and Chicken in Pernod over Almond Chive Rice (recipe below).

Serves 4

Almond-Chive Rice

¼ cup	toasted, flaked almonds	60 mL
2 cups	cooked brown rice	500 mL
3 tbsp.	nonfat sour cream	45 mL
4 tbsp.	minced chives	60 mL
2 tbsp.	amaretto liqueur	30 mL
	salt and freshly ground pepper	

Method Combine all ingredients and press into well-buttered 4-oz. (125 mL) ramekin dishes or muffin cups. Bake in 350°F (180°C) oven about 10 minutes. Cool slightly and unmold.

Serves 4

Main Course

Fragrant Spice-Crusted Pork with Mango Chutney Sauce, page 129
Caramelized Onions, page 130
Mango Carrots with Pine Nuts, page 90

Rustic Picnic Loaf with Rosemary Chicken

We took this picnic loaf and a bottle of cold champagne on a romantic get-away to our favorite down-town hotel – perfect!

Herb Bread:

2½ cups	flour	625 mL
1 tsp.	salt	5 mL
1 tbsp.	instant yeast	15 mL
2 tbsp.	sugar	30 mL
1 tbsp.	chopped fresh basil	15 mL
1 tbsp.	chopped fresh rosemary	15 mL
1¼ cups	warm water (approx.)	300 mL
2 tbsp.	olive oil	30 mL

Rosemary Chicken:

½ cup	chicken stock	125 mL
3	garlic cloves, minced	3
4	single, boneless, chicken breasts	4
½	purple onion, diced	½
1	red pepper, sliced	1
2	carrots, peeled and cut in strips	2
1	small zucchini, thinly sliced	1
½ cup	sun-dried tomatoes	125 mL
1 tbsp.	snipped fresh rosemary	15 mL
1 tbsp.	cornstarch, dissolved in additional chicken stock	15 mL
	salt and pepper to taste	
	olive oil	
	basil and extra rosemary (optional)	

Method

Herb Bread: In a processor, mix dry ingredients and herbs. Slowly add water and oil and process until smooth dough forms, about 3 minutes. If too dry, add more water; if too moist add more flour. Place dough in oiled bowl and oil top of dough. Cover dough with plastic wrap and let rise until doubled in bulk, about 1 hour.

Rosemary Chicken: Meanwhile, in a large skillet, heat stock; add garlic and sliced chicken. Cook on medium heat, turning chicken until no longer pink inside. Add vegetables and rosemary. Simmer about 5 minutes. Stir in cornstarch dissolved in stock and stir until thickened. If too thick, add additional stock, or add light cream for a richer sauce. Season with salt and pepper and more basil and rosemary, if desired. Cool.

Roll dough into 12" (30 cm) round. Pile chicken, vegetables and sauce in center of dough. Bring up sides of dough to form a knot at the top. Place on oiled baking sheet. Brush loaf with olive oil and sprinkle with rosemary. Bake in 350°F (180°C) oven about 30 minutes.

Serves 2-4

Boned Citrus-Glazed Turkey with Cranberry Sausage Stuffing

12-20 lb.	turkey, boned	5.5-9 kg
1	lemon, halved	1
	salt and pepper	

Cranberry Sausage Stuffing:

1 cup	EACH chopped celery and onion	250 mL
¼ cup	butter	60 mL
8 oz.	sausage meat, cooked, drained and crumbled	250 g
4 cups	coarse dry bread crumbs	1 L
1½ cups	cranberries	375 mL
1 tbsp.	EACH minced fresh thyme, rosemary and sage or 1 tsp. (5 mL) dry	15 mL 15 mL
	salt and pepper	
1½ cups	chicken stock	375 mL
1	egg	1
¾ cup	Seville orange marmalade	175 mL
2 tbsp.	orange brandy	30 mL
1 tsp.	soy sauce	5 mL
1 tsp.	ground ginger	5 mL
1	orange, sliced	1
1 cup	orange juice	250 mL
1 tbsp.	cornstarch	15 mL
¼ cup	cold water	60 mL

Method Place boned turkey on flat surface. Rub with lemon. Sprinkle with salt and pepper.

Stuffing: Sauté onion and celery in butter until tender. Pour into a large bowl. Add sausage, bread crumbs, cranberries and seasoning. Whisk egg and chicken broth together and stir into crumb mixture.

Place stuffing along the long edge and roll up. Tie at intervals with string. Mix together marmalade, brandy, soy sauce and ginger. Brush over turkey roll. Top with orange slices. Roast 2-3 hours at 375°F (190°C).

Remove turkey from the pan, pour off excess fat, stir orange juice into the pan and heat. Dissolve cornstarch in water and stir into pan. Cook and whisk until thickened. Season with salt and pepper. Slice turkey roll and arrange on platter with orange slices. Serve with gravy.

Serves 8-12

Boned Turkey Breast with Apricot Stuffing

Apricot Stuffing:

7 tbsp.	diced, dried apricots	105 mL
3½ tbsp.	currants	52 mL
6 tbsp.	butter	90 mL
½	medium onion, diced	½
6 tbsp.	slivered almonds	90 mL
2	tart, green apples, peeled, cored, diced	2
2¼ cups	dry crumbs	550 mL
½ tsp.	salt	2 mL
¼ tsp.	sage	1 mL
3-4 tbsp.	chicken stock	45-60 mL
1	large turkey breast, boned, or 2 boned chickens	1
4	pieces bacon	4
	paprika	

Method

Soak apricots and currents in boiling water to cover, until soft and plumped, about 15 minutes. Drain. Melt 1 tbsp. (15 mL) butter over medium heat. Add onion and cook until soft. Drain. Melt another tablespoon (15 mL) of butter, add almonds and toss 2-3 minutes until golden. Drain. Melt 2 tbsp. (15 mL) butter, add apples and cook until soft, about 5 minutes. Drain. Combine apricots and currents, onions, almonds, apples, bread crumbs, salt and sage. Blend in 3 tbsp. (45 mL) chicken stock or more if needed. Cool completely.

Butterfly turkey breast so meat lays flat. Spread filling on boned meat and roll up jelly-roll style. Tie at intervals with string. Wrap bacon pieces around. Rub turkey with remaining butter. Sprinkle with paprika.

Bake at 350°F (180°C) about 1 hour and 15 minutes.

Serves

6-8

Pictured on page 87.

Boned Turkey Breast with Sweet Italian Sausage and Apple Stuffing

½ cup	melted butter	125 mL
1	large turkey breast, boned*	1
	salt and pepper	

Sweet Italian Sausage and Apple Stuffing:

1 lb.	sweet Italian sausage	500 g
2 tbsp.	butter	30 mL
1 cup	chopped green apples	250 mL
1 cup	minced onions	250 mL
2 cups	fresh bread crumbs	500 mL
½ cup	minced parsley	125 mL
½ cup	sour cream	125 mL
½ cup	chopped fresh sage	125 mL
	salt and freshly ground pepper	

Method

Lay a large piece of cheesecloth on a flat surface and brush with melted butter. Butterfly turkey breast so meat lays flat. Do this without cutting through skin. Place on the buttered cheesecloth, skin side down. Brush with butter and season with salt and pepper. Prepare stuffing.

Stuffing: Steam sausages in shallow boiling water for about 5 minutes. Drain. Peel off skins and chop coarsely. In large skillet, sauté apples and onions in butter about 10 minutes. Add sausages and sauté 5 minutes longer. Place in large bowl and add crumbs, parsley, sour cream and seasonings.

Spoon stuffing over turkey breast and bring up ends of cheesecloth to enclose the meat and stuffing. Tie both ends with kitchen twine. Brush the entire cheesecloth bundle with melted butter. Place skin side up in roasting pan and bake at 325°F (160°C) for 2-3 hours, basting regularly. A meat thermometer works well for this. Remove from pan and let rest for 20 minutes. Carefully remove cheesecloth and slice.

Serves

6-8

*A whole boned turkey or large boned roasting chicken can be substituted for the large turkey breast.

Boneless Turkey Breast Wrapped in Phyllo Pastry with Green Peppercorn Sauce

The ideal intimate turkey dinner for a small group – or for two.

2 tbsp.	butter	30 mL
2	garlic cloves, minced	2
4	boneless turkey fillets	4
8	sheets phyllo pastry	8
½ cup	melted butter	125 mL
1 cup	dry bread crumbs	250 mL
⅓ cup	white wine	75 mL
1 cup	cream	250 mL
	Green Peppercorn Sauce, see page 119*	1
2 tbsp.	Dijon mustard	30 mL
1 tbsp.	chives	15 mL
	melted butter	
	paprika	

Method

In a large skillet, sauté the butter and garlic on low heat. Add turkey breast and sauté on both sides about 10 minutes.

Meanwhile, prepare the phyllo pastry. Take 1 sheet pastry and brush with melted butter. Sprinkle with crumbs. Repeat 7 times with remaining sheets, butter and crumbs. Cover with a towel. Preheat oven to 375°F (190°C).

Remove turkey fillets from skillet and set aside. To the skillet, add the wine, cream and Green Peppercorn Sauce. Whisk until smooth, then add mustard and chives. If sauce is too thick, add more wine or cream. Return turkey to skillet, coating well.

Arrange turkey fillets on edge of phyllo pastry. Spoon sauce over, reserving some for later. Roll up pastry from the short edge, jelly-roll style, tucking in edges. Brush with melted butter and sprinkle with paprika. Place roll on cookie sheet and bake for about 35 minutes. Pass additional sauce.

Serves

2-4

*Use only the green peppercorns for this sauce.

Turkey Scaloppine with Marsala Mushrooms

Marsala, an Italian fortified wine, adds a smoky flavor to this rich mushroom sauce.

6 tbsp.	butter	90 mL
3 cups	sliced mushrooms	750 mL
1 tsp.	crumbled dried thyme	5 mL
1 tsp.	fresh lemon juice	5 mL
	salt and pepper	
½ cup	dry Marsala	125 mL
1½ cups	chicken stock	375 mL
8 x 3 oz.	turkey breast cutlets	8 x 85 mL
	all-purpose flour	
	chopped fresh chives or green onion tops	

Method

Heat 2 tbsp. (30 mL) butter in large heavy skillet over medium heat. Add mushrooms, thyme and lemon juice. Season with salt and pepper. Sauté until mushrooms are golden brown, about 6 minutes. Add Marsala and boil 3 minutes. Add stock and reduce by half, about 12 minutes. Remove and set aside.

Heat 2 tbsp. (30 mL) butter in large heavy skillet over medium heat. Dredge turkey cutlets in flour, tap off excess. Add turkey to skillet and cook just until cooked through, about 2 minutes per side. Transfer to plates and keep warm.

Return sauce to heat. Bring to simmer and whisk in remaining 2 tbsp. (30 mL) butter. Season to taste with salt and pepper. Pour sauce over turkey. Sprinkle with chives and serve.

Serves

4

* If Marsala is not available use sherry as a substitute.

Fragrant Spice-Crusted Pork with Mango Chutney Sauce

Fragrant Spice Mixture:

5	whole cloves	5
1 tsp.	black peppercorns	5 mL
½ tsp.	cumin seeds	2 mL
½	stick cinnamon, broken in half	½
¼ tsp.	dried crushed red pepper	1 mL
1 tsp.	whole coriander seeds	5 mL
½ tsp.	fennel seeds	2 mL
¼ tsp.	ground cardamom	1 mL
2	pork tenderloins (about 1½ lbs. [750 g] in total), trimmed	2
	salt	

Mango Chutney Sauce:

1 cup	mayonnaise	250 mL
1 tbsp.	wine vinegar	15 mL
½ cup	mango chutney	125 mL
1 tbsp.	curry powder	15 mL

Method

Spice Mixture: Heat small heavy skillet over medium heat. Add spice mixture to skillet. Roast, uncovered, until spices are fragrant and darken slightly, shaking pan occasionally, about 2 minutes. Cool slightly. Transfer spices to spice or coffee grinder. Add cardamom and coarsely grind spices. This can be prepared 3 days ahead. Store spice mixture in jar at room temperature.

Preheat barbecue to medium-high heat. Season pork generously with salt. Place spice mixture in shallow dish. Add pork and roll to coat all surfaces with spice mixture. Grill pork until cooked through, about 5 minutes per side. Let set 5 minutes. Cut into medallions and serve with Mango Chutney Sauce or Mango Chutney.

Mango Chutney Sauce: Combine all ingredients and mix well; chill.

Serves

4

Pictured on page 121.

Barbecued Pork Loin with Caramelized Onions and Grilled Pineapple

The onions are caramelized in orange juice – who needs butter?

2 cups	orange juice or more	500 mL
¼ cup	white vinegar	60 mL
1 tbsp.	honey	15 mL
3 tbsp.	soy sauce	45 mL
	black pepper	
6	boneless, lean pork loin chops	6
1	fresh pineapple, peeled and sliced	1
2	large sweet onions, sliced	2

Method For marinade, combine 1 cup (250 mL) juice, vinegar, honey, soy sauce and pepper. Marinate pork, covered, overnight if possible. Heat barbecue to medium and grill pork about 10 minutes on each side, brushing with marinade. For the last 5 minutes, grill pineapple, brushing with marinade.

Caramelized Onions: Place onions in a large heavy skillet with the other cup (250 mL) of orange juice. Cook on medium heat about 15 minutes, stirring often. Onions will caramelize, but may require more juice.

To serve, place a ring of pineapple on each plate. Top with onions. Slice pork in strips and lay across onions.

Serves 6

Caramelized Onions pictured on page 121.

Maple-Mustard & Pecan Roasted Ham

¼ cup	Dijon mustard	60 mL
2 tbsp.	Each honey and maple syrup	60 mL
1 tbsp.	molasses	15 mL
2	small garlic cloves, minced	2
½ cup	pecans, toasted	125 mL
3 tbsp.	fresh bread crumbs	45 mL
1 tsp.	minced fresh rosemary	5 mL
1	large bone-in ham, scored	1

Method Preheat oven to 375°F (190°C). Mix first 5 ingredients in bowl; set aside. Blend pecans, bread crumbs and rosemary in processor until mixture resembles fine meal. Spread mustard mixture all over ham. Arrange ham fat side up and sprinkle nut mixture all over. Roast at 350°F (180°C) for 1 hour. Serve with Sweet Potato Mango Chutney, page 58.

Serves 10-12

Mustard-Coated New York Steak with Horseradish Sauce

2 tbsp.	Dijon mustard	30 mL
1 tbsp.	chopped fresh sage	15 mL
1 tbsp.	chopped fresh thyme	15 mL
2 tbsp.	coarse mustard	30 mL
2 x 1"	thick New York steaks	2 x 2.5 cm
	(about 16 oz. [500 g] each)	
	freshly ground pepper	
	oil	
	salt	
	minced fresh parsley	

Horseradish Sauce:

1 cup	unsalted beef stock	250 mL
1 cup	whipping cream	250 mL
2	fresh thyme sprigs	2
1 tsp.	(or more) prepared horseradish	5 mL

Method Put first 4 ingredients in small bowl. Place steaks on baking sheet. Rub mustard mixture over both sides of steaks. Season generously with pepper. Cover steaks and let stand for 1 hour at room temperature.

Horseradish Sauce: Boil stock, cream and thyme in a medium-sized heavy saucepan until reduced to sauce consistency, about 8 minutes. Mix in 1 tsp. (5 mL) horseradish. Taste, adding more horseradish if desired. Set horseradish sauce aside.

Preheat barbecue to medium high. Brush steaks with oil and season with salt. Grill steaks to desired doneness, about 5 minutes per side for medium-rare. Transfer steaks to plates. Bring Horseradish Sauce to a simmer. Spoon over steaks. Sprinkle with parsley and serve.

Serves 2

Roast Prime Rib with Red Wine Pepper Sauce

3 tbsp.	coarse pickling salt	45 mL
1 tbsp.	coarsely ground pepper	15 mL
2	garlic cloves, finely chopped	2
3-5 rib	prime rib or baron of beef	3-5 rib
4	carrots, coarsely chopped	4
4	celery stalks, coarsely chopped	4
1	fennel bulb, coarsely chopped	1
1	onion, coarsely chopped	1
	fresh thyme sprigs	
2	bay leaves	2

Red Wine Pepper Sauce:

1	large onion, finely chopped	1
1	red pepper, finely chopped	1
1	green pepper, finely chopped	1
2 tbsp.	whole black peppercorns	30 mL
1	bay leaf	1
3	large garlic cloves, finely chopped	3
4 tbsp.	chopped fresh herbs (basil, thyme, etc.)	60 mL
1½ cups	red wine	375 mL
2 cups	beef stock	500 mL
	salt and freshly ground pepper to taste	

Method Combine salt, pepper and garlic; rub mixture all over meat. Spread vegetables, thyme and bay leaves in bottom of roasting pan and place meat on top. Roast at 350°F (180°C) for about 2 hours. Baste frequently.

Red Wine Pepper Sauce: Discard cooked vegetables from roasting pan, reserving about 1 tbsp. (15 mL) drippings. Add the fresh vegetables and sauté until lightly browned, 3-5 minutes. Add peppercorns, bay leaves, garlic and herbs; sauté another 2 minutes. Add wine; stir and scrape brown bits from pan. Add stock and bring to a boil, reducing to half, about 20 minutes. Season with salt. Remove the bay leaf. Serve the prime rib with Red Wine Pepper Sauce and with Red Onion Marmalade (recipe follows).

Serves 6-8

Roast Prime Rib
Continued

Red Onion Marmalade:

1 cup	thinly sliced red onion	250 mL
1 tbsp.	olive oil	15 mL
¼ cup	dry red wine	60 mL
¼ cup	cranberry juice	60 mL

Method Cook red onion in oil over medium heat until onion is very soft and starts to brown. Add wine and juice and boil gently until thick. You may wish to double recipe. Keeps refrigerated for 2 weeks.

Makes about 1½ cups (375 mL)

Filet Mignon with Whisky Sauce

2	slices French bread (1" [2.5 cm]) thick	2
2	beef tenderloin steaks (1" [2.5 cm])	2
1 tbsp.	butter	15 mL
1 tsp.	Dijon mustard	5 mL
1 tbsp.	flour	15 mL
1	shallot, minced	1
3 tbsp.	strong beef stock	45 mL
¼ cup	cream	60 mL
1 tbsp.	chopped parsley	15 mL
4 tbsp.	whisky	60 mL
1 tbsp.	lemon juice	15 mL

Method Cut bread into rounds the same size and shape as the steaks. Heat butter in heavy pan, add mustard and mix well. Brush bread on both sides with mustard butter, place on tray and bake in 350°F (180°C) oven until golden brown.

Add steaks to pan and quickly sauté on both sides. Remove from pan; keep warm. Add flour and shallot to pan. Stir in remaining ingredients and whisk until creamy and thickened, about 2 minutes. Remove bread from oven. Place bread on individual plates and set steaks on bread rounds. Spoon remaining sauce over.

Serves 2

Roast Tenderloin of Beef in Black Pepper

1 cup	black peppercorns	250 mL
4½ lbs.	beef tenderloin (about 2" [5 cm] thick), trimmed	2 kg
	salt	
8 tbsp.	unsalted butter	125 mL
½ cup	cognac	125 mL

Method

It's important to start cooking the meat at least 1 hour before serving so that it will have time to rest, allowing the juices to coagulate in the meat before cutting it. Otherwise, the juices and all their flavor are lost when the meat is cut. About 1¼ hours in advance, preheat the oven to 500°F (260°C).

Meanwhile, wrap the peppercorns in a dishcloth and crush them with a wooden mallet or the bottom of a heavy skillet. Place the crushed peppercorns on a large plate. Season the meat with salt on all sides, then roll it in the crushed pepper, coating all of the surfaces of the meat completely.

Melt 2 tbsp. (30 mL) butter over high heat in a roasting pan just large enough to hold the meat. When the butter begins to sizzle, add the beef and sear quickly on all sides. Place in preheated oven for about 30 minutes, turning once. Determine cooking time by the thickness of meat and degree of doneness you prefer. (4½ lbs. [2 kg] for 30 minutes would be rare to medium rare.) Test for doneness by using a meat thermometer or slice meat through the center.

When the meat has cooked to desired doneness, place on a small plate inverted onto a large plate This allows the meat to rest without sitting in its juices. Cover with foil and place in the oven with heat off to keep warm.

Pour off the collected fat in the roasting pan and add cognac to the pan to deglaze. Place over very low heat, being careful not to ignite cognac. Stir with a wooden spoon to dislodge the bits of meat and pepper that stick to the bottom of the pan. Just before serving, pour juice from meat into the pan and whisk in the butter a bit at a time. Pour into a gravy boat. Quickly cut meat into ½" (1.3 cm) thick slices, arrange on platter and serve with the sauce.

Serves

8 (about 1½ lbs. [750 g] would be perfect for 2)

Spinach-Stuffed Beef Filet Lyonnaise with Lobster Kariba

A decadent splurge!

Red Wine Marinade:

1 cup	olive oil	250 mL
¾ cup	red wine vinegar	175 mL
1 tbsp.	thyme	15 mL
1 tbsp.	minced garlic	15 mL
1 tbsp.	minced parsley	15 mL
1 tsp.	black pepper	5 mL
2 lbs.	beef tenderloin	1 kg
	freshly ground pepper	

Mushroom Spinach Stuffing:

¼ cup	butter	60 mL
1	medium onion, chopped	1
1	garlic clove, minced	1
8-10	mushrooms, sliced	8-10
8 oz.	spinach, chopped	250 g
¾ cup	bread crumbs	175 mL
1	egg	1
¼ cup	red wine	60 mL

Method

Marinade: Combine olive oil, vinegar, herbs and spices in shallow dish. Add beef and marinate for about 1 hour.

Stuffing: Meanwhile, melt butter and sauté onions, garlic and mushrooms. Combine spinach, bread crumbs, egg and red wine. Combine with sautéed vegetables. Flatten and butterfly beef. Spread filling over surface and tie closed. Season with lots of pepper. Bake at 425°F (220°C) about 30-40 minutes. Serve with Lobster Kariba, page 136.

Serves   4

*L*obster *Kariba*

2 tbsp.	chopped shallots	30 mL
1 cup	sliced mushrooms	250 mL
¼ cup	butter	60 mL
1 tsp.	aniseed or fennel	5 mL
	salt and pepper	
4 tbsp.	Pernod	60 mL
¼ cup	chopped fresh parsley	60 mL
1 tbsp.	tomato paste	15 mL
1 cup	whipping cream	250 mL
2 cups	chopped lobster	500 mL

Method: Sauté shallots and mushrooms in butter. Add remaining ingredients, except lobster. Simmer until thickened. Stir in lobster pieces and simmer just until lobster is cooked. Serve with beef, page 135.

Serves 4

*G*rilled *Tequila Salmon*

Use the rest of your tequila for margaritas!

Lime Tequila Marinade:

½ cup	olive oil	125 mL
6 tbsp.	lime juice	90 mL
6 tbsp.	tequila	90 mL
2	jalapeño peppers, minced	2
2 tbsp.	lime zest	30 mL
2 tsp.	chili powder	10 mL
2 tsp.	sugar	10 mL
1 tsp.	coarse salt	5 mL
2-3 lb.	salmon fillet	1-1.5 kg
2 tbsp.	butter	30 mL
	lime zest and slices	

Method Mix marinade ingredients in bowl; let stand 15 minutes or longer. Marinate salmon in mixture for 1 hour. Drain. Place salmon, skin-side down, on a large piece of greased foil. Place over low heat on barbecue, with lid closed, for 10 minutes. Brush generously with marinade. Close lid and turn heat to medium. Grill about 15 minutes longer. Meanwhile, boil remaining marinade in heavy saucepan about 5 minutes. Whisk in butter. Drizzle over grilled salmon. Garnish with lime zest and lime slices.

Serves 4

Chilean Bass with Fruit Salsa

If you haven't tried Chilean Bass – start here – it's very much like lobster.

4	thick pieces Chilean Bass	4
1 tbsp.	olive oil	15 mL
1 tbsp.	lemon juice	15 mL
	Cajun blackening spice (for sodium-restricted diets, choose a brand of spicy natural herbs such as Mrs. Dash)	

Method Brush bass with oil and lemon juice on both sides. Sprinkle a generous amount of seasoning on each side. Spray upper grill of barbecue with a nonstick coating. Cook fish on high about 8 minutes on each side. Serve with Fruit Salsa (below).

Serves 4

Fruit Salsa

1	fresh mango, peeled and chopped or 14 oz. (398 mL) can of sliced mango	1
1 cup	pineapple chunks, fresh or canned	250 mL
1	fresh papaya, peeled and sliced	1
½	purple onion, chopped	½
½	bunch fresh cilantro, chopped	½
1	red pepper, chopped	1
1	green pepper, chopped	1
1 tsp.	pepper flakes (optional)	5 mL
	black pepper	

Method In processor, combine and chop all ingredients, using on and off pulse. Do not over process. Chill.

Makes about 4 cups (1 L)

Succulent Seafood Risotto with Sun-Dried Tomatoes and Spinach

This looks splendid cooked and served in a large paella pan.

2 lbs.	fresh clams	1 kg
2 lbs.	fresh mussels	1 kg
4 cups	chicken stock	1 L
½ cup	chopped sun-dried tomatoes	125 mL
1 tbsp.	olive oil	15 mL
½ cup	finely chopped onion	125 mL
1½ cups	Arborio* or short-grain rice	375 mL
½ cup	white wine	125 mL
6 cups	torn fresh spinach	1.5 L
1 tsp.	saffron threads	5 mL
1 lb.	prawns	500 g
½ lb.	scallops	250 g
	salt and pepper to taste	
3 tbsp.	fresh Parmesan cheese	45 mL
	chopped fresh parsley	

Method

Steam clams and mussels until shells open, about 10 minutes. Set aside.

Bring chicken stock to a simmer. Combine tomatoes and ½ cup (125 mL) broth in a bowl, cover and set aside. Keep remaining broth warm.

Heat oil in large paella-style pan. Add onion and sauté about 3 minutes. Add rice and cook about 2 minutes, stirring constantly. Add wine, stirring until absorbed. Add remaining broth ½ cup (125 mL) at a time, stirring constantly, about 20 minutes cooking time. Add tomato mixture, spinach and saffron, stirring and cooking about 5 minutes. Add prawns and scallops, cooking just until opaque. Season with salt and pepper. Spoon clams and mussels over, tossing slightly. Sprinkle with cheese and chopped parsley.

Serves

6-8

*Arborio rice is ideal for risotto because it has more starch than regular short-grained rice.

Pictured on opposite page.

Main Course

Succulent Seafood Risotto with
  Sun-Dried Tomatoes and Spinach, page 138

Vegetable Schnitzel with Béarnaise, Crab and Asparagus

Vegetable Schnitzel:

½ lb.	broccoli, chopped	250 g
½ lb.	zucchini, chopped	250 g
½ lb.	green beans, chopped	250 g
1	onion, finely chopped	1
1	garlic clove, minced	1
2 cups	dry bread crumbs	500 mL
¼ cup	all-purpose flour	60 mL
2 tbsp.	milk	30 mL
	salt and freshly ground pepper	
	vegetable oil	

Béarnaise (low-fat style):

¼ cup	white wine vinegar	60 mL
1 tbsp.	chopped shallots	15 mL
1 tbsp.	tarragon	15 mL
	freshly ground pepper	
3	egg whites	3
1 tbsp.	Dijon mustard	15 mL
4 tbsp.	hot, melted light margarine	60 mL
2	crab claws or 4 oz. (113 g) canned crab for garnish	2
	asparagus for garnish	

Method Cook broccoli, zucchini and green beans in a large saucepan of boiling salted water until tender. Drain well. Purée vegetables in blender with onion and garlic. Transfer to large bowl. Mix in bread crumbs and flour. Stir in milk. Season with salt and pepper. Refrigerate mixture until well chilled, about 30 minutes. Form mixture into 3" (7 cm) balls. Flatten into oval patties. These can be prepared 1 day ahead. Refrigerate.

Béarnaise: Boil the first 4 ingredients until reduced to about 2 tbsp. (30 mL). Strain. Place the egg whites in a processor or blender with Dijon. Blend until thick and creamy. With machine running, add the strained vinegar mixture, then slowly add hot margarine. Blend until thick.

Heat ¾" (2 cm) oil in a large heavy skillet over high heat. Add patties and cook until brown, about 3 minutes per side. Drain on paper towels. Serve patties with Béarnaise Sauce. Top with crab and asparagus.

Serves 4

Crab and Spinach Torte

3 cups	your favorite bread stuffing	750 mL
2	eggs, lightly beaten	2
2	onions, chopped	2
2	garlic cloves, minced	2
2 tbsp.	butter	30 mL
2 x 10 oz.	pkgs. frozen spinach, thawed, well drained	2 x 283 g
2 cups	shredded mozzarella	500 mL
2 cups	crab chunks	500 mL
1	small red pepper, cut in strips (can use mushrooms as well)	1
	salt and freshly ground pepper to taste	
8	eggs, lightly beaten	8
4	tomatoes, sliced	4

Method Prepare stuffing. When cooled stir in 2 eggs. Press into 8" (20 cm) spring-form pan. Sauté onions and garlic in butter until tender. Remove from heat, stir in spinach. Sprinkle half of cheese over crust, then half of the crab. Top with half of spinach, sliced peppers, remaining cheese and final layer of spinach. Add salt and pepper to beaten eggs. Pour eggs over all. Top with tomato slices. Bake at 400°F (200°C) for 40-45 minutes, or until set. Sprinkle with remaining crab.

Cool 5-10 minutes before cutting.

Serves 6-8

Desserts

Caramel Apple Cheesecake with Peaches

Another of my "to-live-for" recipes. Nothing to weigh you down here!

Cinnamon Sugar Crust:

1 cup	graham cracker crumbs	250 mL
3 tbsp.	light margarine, melted	45 mL
3 tbsp.	brown sugar	45 mL
1 tbsp.	cinnamon	15 mL

Caramel Apple Filling:

½ cup	brown sugar	125 mL
3 tbsp.	water	45 mL
2 cups	peeled, sliced tart green apples	500 mL
1 cup	peeled, sliced peaches	250 mL
8 oz.	light cream cheese	250 g
8 oz.	quark cheese	250 g
½ cup	sugar	125 mL
2 tbsp.	cornstarch	30 mL
1 tbsp.	cinnamon	15 mL
3	eggs	3
1 cup	nonfat sour cream	250 mL
2 tbsp.	brown sugar	30 mL
1 tsp.	vanilla	5 mL

Method

Crust: Mix crumbs, margarine, sugar and cinnamon together and press into nonstick-oil-sprayed 8" (20 cm) springform pan. Bake in 350°F (180°C) oven 10 minutes.

Filling: In heavy skillet stir together brown sugar and water. Over medium heat bring to a boil, then simmer on low heat 5 minutes. Add apples and peaches and toss to coat with caramel. Spoon fruit onto crust, reserving a few slices for the top. To prepare cheesecake filling, beat together the cheeses, sugar, cornstarch and cinnamon. Add the eggs 1 at a time. Beat well for about 2 minutes. Pour filling over fruit. Reduce oven to 325°F (160°C) and bake cheesecake about 45 minutes. Meanwhile, mix together sour cream, sugar and vanilla. When cheesecake is finished baking, spoon sour cream mixture across top and bake 10 more minutes. Cake should be quite firm at this point; if not, bake an extra 10 minutes. When cool, spoon reserved fruit on top to decorate. Chill at least 4 hours or overnight.

Serves 6-8

Mile-High Mango Cheesecake with Kiwi Coulis

Macadamia Coconut Crust:

1 cup	coconut	250 mL
3.5 oz.	macadamia nuts	100 g
	(reserve 10 nuts for top)	
½ cup	sliced almonds	125 mL
3 tbsp.	brown sugar	45 mL
3 tbsp.	butter	45 mL

Mango Filling:

3 tbsp.	gelatin (3 x 7 g env.)	45 mL
½ cup	water	125 mL
½ cup	lime juice	125 mL
6	egg yolks	6
1 cup	sugar	250 mL
⅓ cup	rum	75 mL
1 cup	mango purée	250 mL
3 x 8 oz.	cream cheese, softened	3 x 250 g
6	egg whites, beaten stiff	6
2 cups	whipping cream, whipped	500 mL

Kiwi Coulis:

6-8	kiwis, peeled	6-8
2 tbsp.	sugar	30 mL
	drop of green food coloring	
	(optional)	
	whipped cream	

Method: **Crust:** To prepare crust, in processor, chop coconut, nuts and brown sugar until crumbly. Add butter. Process on and off. Pat into 10" (25 cm) springform pan. Bake at 375°F (190°C) for 10 minutes. Cool.

Filling: Sprinkle gelatin on water and lime juice in a small bowl. Heat in microwave 1 minute on medium heat. Beat egg yolks, sugar and rum until thick and creamy. Beat into mango purée and cream cheese. Continue beating. Gently fold in beaten egg whites and whipped cream. Pour into crust. Chill at least 4 hours.

Kiwi Coulis: Combine all ingredients and process until smooth.

Unmold cheesecake and decorate with sweetened whipped cream and reserved macadamia nuts. Spoon Kiwi Coulis on plates and set wedges of cheesecake on top.

Serves 10-12

Ultra-Light – Ultimate Cheesecake

This is everything a wonderful cheesecake should be, creamy, high and sinfully rich but without the weigh-you-down heaviness because it is low-fat!

Cinnamon Crust:

1½ cups	low-fat cinnamon cookie crumbs	375 mL
3 tbsp.	light margarine	45 mL

Filling:

8 oz.	light cream cheese	250 g
16 oz.	skim ricotta cheese	1 kg
½ cup	sugar	125 mL
2	eggs	2
2	egg whites	2
3 tbsp.	cornstarch	45 mL
1 tbsp.	vanilla	15 mL

Topping:

1½ cups	nonfat sour cream	375 mL
3 tbsp.	sugar	45 mL
1 tsp.	vanilla	5 mL

Method

Crust: Mix crumbs and margarine and press into 8" (20 cm) springform pan, sprayed with a nonstick spray. Bake at 350°F (180°C) for 10 minutes. Cool.

Filling: Beat together cheeses and sugar until light and fluffy. Add eggs and whites and beat about 5 minutes. Beat in cornstarch and vanilla until well mixed. Pour onto baked crust. Lower oven to 335°F (170°C) and bake about 50 minutes.

Topping: Combine topping ingredients. When cheesecake is baked, spoon topping across top and return to the oven for 10 minutes. Chill at least 4 hours or overnight.

Serve this cheesecake with a very intensely flavored fruit purée such as blackberry, raspberry or mango. Tinned mango slices or purée work very nicely.

Serves

10-12

Pictured on the back cover.

*Fruit Purée: To make a fruit purée, blend fresh or canned fruit in a blender or food processor until smooth; add sugar to taste, if necessary.

$\mathcal{L}$ight Lemon Cheesecake

Granola Crust:

1 cup	low-fat granola	250 mL
2 tbsp.	brown sugar	30 mL
1 tbsp.	grated lemon zest	15 mL
4 tsp.	butter, at room temperature	20 mL

Lemon Filling:

1½ cups	lemon yogurt	375 mL
1½ cups	ricotta cheese	375 mL
1 cup	cream cheese	250 mL
4 tsp.	cornstarch	20 mL
2 tsp.	vanilla	10 mL
6	eggs	6
1 cup	sugar	250 mL
1 tbsp.	grated lemon zest	15 mL
	sliced fresh strawberries, for garnish	

Method

Crust: Combine granola, sugar, and zest in processor and process until fine. Add butter and process until mixture holds together. Pat into bottom of a 9" (23 cm) springform pan. Bake at 350°F (180°C) for 10 minutes. Meanwhile, prepare the filling.

Filling: Purée the yogurt, cheeses, cornstarch and vanilla in the processor. Add eggs, sugar and lemon zest. Process until smooth. Pour into the crust after it has baked for 10 minutes. Set on a baking sheet and bake until set, approximately 50-60 minutes more.

Cool and garnish with sliced fresh strawberries.

Serves

8-10

Chocolate-Mocha Cheesecake

16 oz.	low-fat small-curd cottage cheese	500 mL
8 oz.	Neufchâtel cheese (reduced-fat cream cheese) at room temperature	250 g
1¼ cups	sugar	300 mL
1 tbsp.	vanilla extract	15 mL
2 tsp.	instant espresso powder or instant coffee powder	10 mL
¼ tsp.	salt	1 mL
3	large eggs, at room temperature	3
6 tbsp.	unsweetened Dutch-process cocoa powder	90 mL

Papaya Strawberry Sauce:

14 oz.	can papaya chunks	398 mL
1 cup	sliced strawberries	250 mL

Method

Position rack in lowest third of oven and preheat to 350°F (180°C). Line bottom of 8" (20 cm) round cake pan with 2" (5 cm) sides with parchment paper. Spray sides of pan with vegetable oil spray.

Blend cottage cheese in processor until silky smooth, scraping down sides occasionally, about 3 minutes. Add Neufchâtel cheese and blend well. Add 1 cup (250 mL) sugar, vanilla extract, espresso powder and salt and blend well. Add eggs and process just until smooth. Pour 2 cups (500 mL) of the coffee batter into a spouted measuring cup. Add cocoa powder and remaining ¼ cup (60 mL) sugar to batter in processor and blend well.

Pour 1¾ cups (425 mL) cocoa batter into the prepared pan. Pour coffee batter directly into center of cocoa batter (coffee batter will fill center, pushing cocoa batter to edge). Pour remaining cocoa batter directly into center of coffee batter. Run small knife through batters to create marbled pattern. Set cake pan into 9 x 13" (23 x 33 cm) baking pan. Pour enough boiling water into baking pan to come halfway up the sides of the cake pan. Set baking pan in oven.

Bake cake until edges just begin to puff and crack and center is just set, about 50 minutes. Remove cake from baking pan and set on rack to cool. Refrigerate cake until ready to serve.

Sauce: Purée sauce ingredients until smooth.

To serve, pour a pool of Papaya Strawberry Sauce on individual plates and position cheesecake slices on sauce.

Serves

8-10

Pictured on the back cover.

Praline Pumpkin Cheesecake

Gingersnap Crust:

1½ cups	finely ground gingersnap cookies	375 mL
¾ cup	ground hazelnuts	175 mL
3 tbsp.	brown sugar	45 mL
6 tbsp.	unsalted butter, melted, cooled	90 mL

Creamy Pumpkin Filling:

1½ lbs.	cream cheese, at room temperature	750 g
1 cup	firmly packed brown sugar	250 mL
1½ cups	canned solid-pack pumpkin	375 mL
½ cup	whipping cream	125 mL
⅓ cup	pure maple syrup	75 mL
1 tbsp.	vanilla extract	15 mL
¾ tsp.	ground cinnamon	3 mL
¼ tsp.	ground allspice	1 mL
4	large eggs	4

Praline Topping:

1¼ cup	sugar	300 mL
6 tbsp.	water	90 mL
1 cup	coarsely chopped toasted hazelnuts	250 mL

Method

Crust: Mix first 3 ingredients in a medium bowl. Add butter and stir until well combined. Press crumb mixture onto bottom and 2" (5 cm) up sides of 9" (23 cm) springform pan with 2¾" (6.5 cm) sides. Bake at 325°F (160°C) for 8 minutes. Cool. Maintain oven temperature.

Filling: Using an electric mixer, beat cream cheese and sugar until fluffy. Beat in pumpkin. Add remaining ingredients, except eggs; beat until smooth. Add eggs, 1 at a time, beating just until combined.

Pour batter into prepared crust. Bake until puffed and center is set, about 1½ hours. (Cheesecake will rise slightly above edge of pan.) Transfer to rack and cool 30 minutes. Run knife around pan sides to loosen cheesecake. Cool completely. Cover and refrigerate overnight or up to 2 days.

Praline: Line cookie sheet with foil. Butter foil. Stir sugar and water in medium-sized heavy saucepan over low heat until sugar dissolves. Increase heat and boil without stirring until syrup turns deep golden brown; brush down sides of pan with wet pastry brush and swirl pan occasionally. Stir in hazelnuts. Immediately pour praline onto cookie sheet; spread to ¼" (6 mm) thickness. Cool. Break praline into 2" (5 cm) pieces.

Transfer cheesecake to platter. Release sides. Arrange praline pieces atop cheesecake. Cut cheesecake into wedges and serve.

Serves 12

Baklava Cheesecake

14-16	sheets phyllo	14-16
1 cup	melted butter or margarine	250 mL
1 cup	crumbs	250 mL

Cream Cheese Filling:

2 x 8 oz.	cream cheese	2 x 250 g
¾ cup	sugar	175 mL
⅓ cup	cornstarch	75 mL
2 tbsp.	butter	30 mL
4	eggs	4
1 cup	whipping cream	250 mL
2 tsp.	vanilla	10 mL
2 tbsp.	lemon juice	30 mL
1 cup	chopped walnuts	250 mL
½ cup	sugar	125 mL
1 tbsp.	cinnamon	15 mL

Syrup:

1 cup	sugar	250 mL
1½ cups	water	375 mL
1 cup	honey	250 mL
2 tbsp.	cinnamon	30 mL
	lemon and orange slices	
	orange zest and walnuts, for garnish	

Method

Line a 10" (25 cm) springform pan with 1 sheet phyllo. Brush with butter, spread with crumbs. Repeat, using 8 sheets of phyllo, letting sheets hang over sides of pan.

Beat first 4 filling ingredients well. Add eggs 1 at a time. Beat in cream, vanilla and lemon juice. Pour filling into pan. Fold phyllo over top; brush with butter. Bake at 350°F (180°C) 50-60 minutes, until firm. Cool.

Meanwhile, place 1 phyllo sheet on greased cookie sheet. Brush with butter. Mix walnuts, sugar and cinnamon and sprinkle on top. Repeat layers with remaining phyllo. Using a sharp knife, cut phyllo into 10" (25 cm) circle. Score into 10 pieces but do not cut through. Bake at 375°F (190°C) for 10-15 minutes. Cool.

While cheesecake is cooling, prepare the syrup; combine all the syrup ingredients and boil for about 10 minutes. Brush the top of cheesecake with syrup, pressing down gently. Pour some syrup over top and set the round of phyllo and walnut pastry on top. Spoon remainder of syrup over cake. Let chill. Decorate with orange zest and walnuts.

Serves

10

Pictured on page 157.

Fried Sweet Cream

It's called fried sweet cream but it's made with milk – semolina helps give the mixture its smooth and creamy texture.

4 cups	milk	1 L
1 cup	sugar	250 mL
1 tbsp.	grated lemon peel	15 mL
	pinch of salt	
1 cup + 2 tbsp.	semolina flour	280 mL
2	large eggs	2
2	eggs, beaten to blend	2
1½ cups	dry bread crumbs	375 mL
3 tbsp.	unsalted butter	45 mL
3 tbsp.	vegetable oil	45 mL
	powdered sugar	

Method

Bring first 4 ingredients to simmer in medium-sized heavy saucepan over medium heat. Gradually stir in semolina. Cook until mixture thickens to consistency of mashed potatoes, stirring frequently, about 10 minutes. Remove saucepan from heat. Beat in 2 eggs.

Sprinkle a baking pan with water. Spoon semolina into pan, spreading with moistened spatula to thickness of 1" (2.5 cm). Cool completely.

Line a large cookie sheet with waxed paper. Cut cooled semolina mixture into 1½" (4 cm) diamonds, using a cookie cutter or knife. Dip each piece into beaten eggs, then coat in bread crumbs. Arrange on prepared sheet. This can be prepared 1 day ahead. Refrigerate semolina diamonds, uncovered.

Melt 1 tbsp. (15 mL) butter with 1 tbsp. (15 mL) oil in a heavy skillet over medium-high heat. Add ⅓ of semolina diamonds and cook until golden brown, about 2 minutes per side. Drain on paper towels. Repeat with remaining butter, oil and semolina diamonds in 2 batches. Arrange on plates. Sprinkle with powdered sugar. Serve warm or at room temperature.

Serves 6

Blackberry Bread Pudding with Chantilly Cream

This fabulous concoction gives bread pudding a whole new meaning.

1	loaf white bread	1
	butter or soft margarine	
4 cups	blackberries	1 L
1 cup	sugar	250 mL
½ cup	blackberry liqueur or brandy	125 mL

Method Remove bread crusts and slice bread. Lightly butter. Use the soft margarine, if preferred, so that it does not harden on bread.

Sprinkle ½ of the sugar into the blackberries.

Butter a springform pan well. Spoon in some of the berries. Line with buttered bread slices and sprinkle on ⅓ of the remaining sugar. Sprinkle with liqueur. Pour in ½ of the berries. Top with more bread slices and press down. Sprinkle more sugar and liqueur over. Top with remaining berries and more liqueur. Press bread slices across top. Sprinkle with remaining sugar and liqueur. Wrap lightly with plastic wrap. Place a stack of plates on top to weigh down. Chill at least 6-8 hours. Remove from pan and serve slices of the Blackberry Bread Pudding with Chantilly Cream (below).

Serves 6-8

Chantilly Cream

1 cup	sour cream	250 mL
¼ cup	Demerara sugar	60 mL
1 cup	whipping cream, whipped	250 mL

Method Mix sour cream and sugar. Fold in whipped cream.

Makes about 3 cups (750 mL)

Grapefruit Sorbet

What a palate cleanser! Serve with mint leaves and sugared grapes.

2 cups	water	500 mL
1 cup	sugar	250 mL
1	peeled, quartered, grapefruit	1
2 cups	grapefruit juice	500 mL

Method Combine water and sugar and boil for 5 minutes. Process grapefruit and juice in food processor until smooth. Add sugar syrup and combine well. Pour into a shallow pan and freeze until firm. Scoop into processor and process until fluffy. Put into a bowl and freeze.

Makes about 1 quart (1 L)

Frozen Caramel Mousse with Butterscotch Sauce

¾ cup	sugar	175 mL
½ cup	boiling water	125 mL
4	egg yolks, at room temperature	4
1½ cups	whipping cream	375 mL
½ tsp.	vanilla	2 mL

Butterscotch Sauce:

¼ cup	brown sugar	60 mL
¼ cup	corn syrup	60 mL
2 tbsp.	butter	30 mL
¼ cup	white sugar	60 mL
¼ cup	whipping cream	60 mL
	pinch of salt	
½ tsp.	vanilla	2 mL

Method Cook sugar in a heavy pan over low heat without stirring, until rich brown. Swirl pan and watch carefully for about 20 minutes. Using a long-handled spoon, slowly stir in boiling water. Cook until caramel dissolves, about 4 minutes. Beat egg yolks until thick and light. Beat in hot caramel slowly and continue until mixture is cool. Cool to room temperature. Beat cream and vanilla to soft peaks and fold into caramel mixture. Pour into a 9" (23 cm) springform pan and freeze until firm.

Sauce: Shortly before serving, prepare sauce. Combine all ingredients, except vanilla, in heavy pan and simmer 5 minutes. Let cool 3 minutes. Blend in vanilla. Spoon over slices of mousse.

Serves 6

Frozen Pumpkin Mousse Torte with Hot Caramel Sauce

Pecan Crust:

3 cups	pecans, toasted (11 oz. [315 g])	750 mL
½ cup	packed golden brown sugar	125 mL
3 tbsp.	butter, melted	45 mL

Filling:

2½ cups	chilled whipping cream	625 mL
1 cup	packed golden brown sugar	250 mL
8	large egg yolks	8
1½ cups	canned solid-pack pumpkin	375 mL
½ cup	light corn syrup	125 mL
3 tbsp.	dark rum	45 mL
1½ tsp.	ground ginger	7 mL
¾ tsp.	ground cinnamon	3 mL
¼ tsp.	ground nutmeg	1 mL

Caramel Rum Sauce:

¼ cup	white sugar	60 mL
¼ cup	brown sugar	60 mL
¼ cup	corn syrup	60 mL
¼ cup	butter	60 mL
¼ cup	whipping cream	60 mL
1 tsp.	vanilla	5 mL
1 tbsp.	rum	15 mL

Method

Crust: Finely chop nuts and sugar in processor. Add butter and blend, using on/off turns, until moist crumbs form. Press mixture onto bottom and all the way up sides of 9" (23 cm) springform pan with 2¾" (6.5 cm) sides, cover completely. Freeze 10 minutes. Bake crust at 350°F (180°C) until golden, about 10 minutes. Cool.

Filling: Whisk 1 cup (250 mL) cream, sugar and yolks in a medium-sized heavy saucepan. Stir constantly over medium heat until candy thermometer registers 160°F (71°C), about 6 minutes. Strain into a large bowl. Using an electric mixer, beat mixture until cool and slightly thickened, about 8 minutes. Beat in pumpkin, corn syrup, rum and spices. Using an electric mixer, beat remaining 1½ cups (375 mL) of cream in a large bowl to medium-stiff peaks. Fold into pumpkin mixture. Transfer filling to crust. Cover and freeze overnight.

Caramel Rum Sauce: Combine first 5 ingredients and microwave on high about 5 minutes, or until thickened. Stir in vanilla and rum. Serve hot sauce on the side.

Serves   12

Frozen Mocha Roca Torte

A big, beautiful dessert that layers chocolate and coffee ice creams with mocha sauce in a macaroon cookie crust.

Mocha Sauce:

2 cups	icing sugar	500 mL
1 cup	cocoa	250 mL
⅓ cup	melted butter	75 mL
¼ cup	hot coffee	60 mL

Macaroon Crust:

3 cups	macaroon cookie crumbs	750 mL
¼ cup	unsalted butter (1 stick), melted	60 mL

Mocha Roca Filling:

1 qt.	chocolate ice cream	1 L
1 qt.	coffee ice cream	1 L
¾ cup	chopped Almond Roca or Heath Bars (about 5 oz. [140 g])	175 mL

Method

Mocha Sauce: Mix together icing sugar and cocoa. Whisk in melted butter and hot coffee until smooth – adding more coffee if too thick to pour.

Crust: Oil 9" (23 cm) springform pan. Mix 2 cups (500 mL) of the crumbs and butter in a medium bowl. Press firmly into bottom of prepared pan. Freeze until firm.

Filling: Soften chocolate ice cream in refrigerator until spreadable but not melted. Spread over crust and smooth top. Freeze until firm. Spoon ½ cup (125 mL) sauce over ice cream and sprinkle with remaining 1 cup (250 mL) cookie crumbs. Freeze until firm.

Soften coffee ice cream in refrigerator until spreadable but not melted. Spread in pan. Smooth surface and freeze until firm. Spread ½ cup (125 mL) sauce over coffee ice cream. Sprinkle with Almond Roca and freeze until firm. This can be prepared 3 days ahead. Cover tightly.

To serve, rewarm remaining sauce over low heat until lukewarm, stirring frequently. Remove pan sides. Cut cake into wedges. Serve, passing warm Mocha Sauce separately.

Serves

10-12

Lemon-Mango-Pistachio Baked Alaska

Not an oz. of fat here! Unbelievable!
This makes a wonderful birthday cake.

1 pint	mango sorbet	500 mL
1 pint	nonfat vanilla frozen yogurt	500 mL
3 tbsp.	lemon zest	45 mL
1	lemon angel food cake, baked	1
8	egg whites	8
¼ tsp.	cream of tartar	1 mL
1 cup	sugar	250 mL
¼ cup	chopped pistachios	60 mL
	lemon zest	

Method

Soften sorbet and yogurt slightly. Fold lemon zest into vanilla yogurt. Slice cake into 3 layers. Spread mango sorbet over bottom layer. Top with next layer of cake. Spread vanilla-lemon yogurt on this layer and top with last layer of cake. Wrap cake and freeze.

Just before serving, beat egg whites with cream of tartar until stiff. Slowly add sugar, beating until a stiff meringue forms. Remove cake from freezer and frost thickly with meringue. If desired, use bag to pipe extra meringue on cake for ornate design. Sprinkle with pistachios. Bake cake in preheated 450°F (230°C) oven about 10 minutes, or until golden brown.
Sprinkle with lemon zest. Serve with a fruit purée if desired, see page 146.

Serves 8-10

Dessert

Baklava Cheesecake, page 150

Chocolate Coconut Phyllo Triangles with Vanilla Ice Cream

Like all phyllo recipes, you can make ahead and freeze prior to baking.

4 oz.	semisweet chocolate, chopped	115 g
¼ cup	sweetened grated coconut, toasted lightly	60 mL
¼ cup	blanched almonds, toasted lightly	60 mL
½ cup	unsalted butter, softened	125 mL
6	sheets phyllo	6
	vanilla ice cream, as accompaniment	

Method

In food processor chop the chocolate finely, add the coconut, the almonds and ½ of the butter, and blend until it is smooth. In a small saucepan melt the remaining butter.

Halve the phyllo lengthwise, stack between 2 sheets of waxed paper and cover with a dampened kitchen towel. Working with 1 strip of phyllo at a time, arrange it on a work surface with a short side facing you. Brush it lightly with butter. Put a heaping tablespoon of the chocolate mixture in the upper right-hand corner of the strip, fold the phyllo in half lengthwise, covering the filling, and brush it lightly with some of the butter. Fold down the top right hand corner of the phyllo to form a triangle and continue to fold the triangle over into itself, side to side (flag-style), maintaining the triangular shape, until the phyllo strip is wrapped completely around the filling. Brush the triangle with some of the remaining butter and transfer it to a baking sheet. Form 11 more triangles with the remaining phyllo and filling in the same manner. The triangles may be prepared, up to this point, 2 weeks in advance and kept well wrapped and frozen.

Bake the triangles in a preheated 400°F (200°C) oven for 8-12 minutes, or until they are golden. Serve them hot with the ice cream.

Makes

12 triangles, to serve 6.

Cottage Bavarian with Brandied Fruit Purée

¼ cup	cold water	60 mL
1½ tsp.	unflavored gelatin	7 mL
¾ cup	plain low-fat yogurt	175 mL
1 cup	low-fat cottage cheese	250 mL
¼ cup	sugar	60 mL
1 tsp.	vanilla	5 mL
2	egg whites, room temperature	2

Brandied Fruit Purée:

1 cup	fruit (berries, peaches, etc.)	250 mL
2 tbsp.	sugar	30 mL
2 tbsp.	brandy	30 mL

Method   Place water in a small heavy saucepan. Sprinkle with gelatin and let stand 5 minutes. Set over very low heat and stir until water is warm and gelatin dissolved, about 30 seconds. Cool slightly. Stir in yogurt. Combine cottage cheese, sugar and vanilla in processor and purée. Transfer to bowl. Stir in yogurt mixture. Beat egg whites until soft peaks form. Stir ¼ of them into cottage cheese mixture to lighten. Gently fold in remaining whites. Spoon into 6, 6-oz. (188 mL) wine glasses. Cover with plastic wrap and refrigerate at least 2 or up to 6 hours before serving.

Sauce: Combine sauce ingredients and purée. Serve over the Bavarian.

Serves   6

White Chocolate Blancmange

An updated treat from the past. Very elegant!

2½ cups	milk	625 mL
¼ cup	cornstarch	60 mL
10 oz.	white chocolate, chopped	285 g
1 tbsp.	vanilla	15 mL
4 oz.	brandy	125 mL
	Brandied Fruit Purée (above)	
	melted dark chocolate (optional)	

Method   Mix ½ cup (125 mL) milk and cornstarch in small bowl. In microwave, heat 2 cups (500 mL) milk on high, about 4 minutes. Mix in white chocolate and stir until melted and smooth. Stir in cornstarch mixture and return to microwave on medium high for about 4 more minutes, checking and stirring. Stir in vanilla and brandy. Pour into molds or ramekin dishes sprayed with a nonstick spray. Chill at least 4 hours. Serve with Brandied Fruit Purée (above). If desired, drizzle with melted dark chocolate. Serve with Lace Biscuits, page 183.

Serves   6

Bittersweet Chocolate Mousse Layered with Orange Brandied Mousse

Bittersweet Chocolate Mousse:

12 oz.	bittersweet chocolate	340 g
1½ tsp.	vanilla	7 mL
1½ cups	whipping cream, heated to boiling	375 mL
2 tbsp.	butter	30 mL
6	egg yolks	6
3	egg whites, stiffly beaten	3

Orange Brandied Mousse:

⅔ cup	boiling water	150 mL
2 tbsp.	gelatin (2 x 7 g env.)	30 mL
½ cup	sugar	125 mL
6 oz.	frozen concentrated orange juice	178 mL
1 cup	whipping cream	250 mL
3 tbsp.	brandy	45 mL
2 cups	ice cubes	500 mL

whipped cream, fresh orange zest,
chocolate curls for garnish

Method   **Bittersweet Chocolate Mousse:** Combine chocolate and vanilla in processor. Mix 30 seconds. Add boiling cream and butter and mix until chocolate is melted. Add yolks. Mix well. Fold in beaten egg whites. Chill.

Orange Brandied Mousse: Pour boiling water and gelatin into a blender. Whirl on high for 30 seconds. Add sugar, blend. Add orange juice, whipping cream and brandy. Blend on high. Add ice cubes and continue blending.

Half fill parfait glasses with Orange Brandied Mousse. Spoon Bittersweet Chocolate Mousse over Orange Brandied Mousse. Chill thoroughly. Decorate with whipped cream, fresh orange zest and chocolate curls.

Serves   6

White Chocolate Macadamia Nut Terrine with Raspberry & Mango Purée

6	egg yolks	6
½ cup	sugar	125 mL
9 oz.	white chocolate, melted	280 g
½ cup	raspberry liqueur	125 mL
1 tbsp.	vanilla	15 mL
2 tbsp.	gelatin, dissolved in	30 mL
⅓ cup	cold water	75 mL
2 cups	whipping cream, whipped	500 mL
1 cup	toasted, chopped macadamia nuts	250 mL
	whipped cream for garnish	
	raspberry purée and mango purée (page 146)	

Method Whisk the yolks and sugar until frothy. Microwave on medium for 2 minutes. Whisk in chocolate, liqueur and vanilla. Heat gelatin and water in microwave 30 seconds on medium. Whisk into chocolate mixture. Fold in whipped cream and nuts. Pour into a plastic-wrap-lined 6-cup (1.5 L) mold. Chill overnight. Unmold and decorate with whipped cream and purées. Serve chilled.

Serves 6-8

Light and Lovely Café Crème Brulée

½ cup	strong coffee	125 mL
10 oz.	low-fat sweetened condensed milk or 13½ oz. (385 mL) evaporated skim milk and ⅔ cup (150 mL) sugar	300 mL
2	eggs	2
2	egg whites	2
2 tbsp.	coffee liqueur	30 mL
4 tbsp.	dark brown sugar	60 mL

Method In large bowl whisk coffee and milk (and sugar if using evaporated milk). Microwave on high until hot, 4-5 minutes. In separate bowl, beat eggs, egg whites and liqueur until well blended. Whisk in hot milk mixture. Pour into 4 oz. (125 mL) custard cups and set in a baking dish half-filled with hot water. Bake at 325°F (160°C) just until set, about 40 minutes. Chill well. Just before serving, spread 1 tbsp. (15 mL) brown sugar on each custard. Broil just until sugar is browned and bubbly.

Serves 4

Raspberry Tiramisu

This is a remake of the classic Italian trifle-type dessert with ladyfingers soaked in raspberry syrup instead of espresso – truly a dessert made in heaven!

3 x 10 oz.	pkgs. frozen unsweetened raspberries	3 x 300 g
16 oz.	mascarpone cheese*	500 g
½ cup	granulated sugar	125 mL
2	egg yolks	2
¼ cup	brandy	60 mL
1 tbsp.	lemon juice	15 mL
1½ tsp.	vanilla	7 mL
2 cups	whipping cream	500 mL
12	small soft ladyfingers, halved, or an 8" (20 cm) pound cake thinly sliced	12
1 tbsp.	unsweetened cocoa powder chocolate curls	15 mL
½ cup	fresh raspberries	125 mL

Method

In a colander set over a bowl, thaw raspberries, reserving juice; set aside.

In a large bowl, beat mascarpone with sugar. In a separate bowl set over hot (not boiling) water, beat egg yolks with clean beaters for 5 minutes, or until pale and thickened; beat into mascarpone mixture. Stir in brandy, lemon juice and vanilla. Whip ½ cup (125 mL) of the cream; fold into mascarpone mixture.

Line bottom of an 8-cup (2 L) glass trifle bowl with 12 ladyfinger halves; brush well with about 3 tbsp. (45 mL) reserved raspberry juice. Spread with ¼ of the mascarpone mixture. Sift 1 tsp. (5 mL) of the cocoa over top. Sprinkle with ⅓ of the thawed raspberries, pressing some against glass to show through.

Repeat mascarpone, cocoa and raspberry layers twice. Cover top raspberry layer with remaining 12 ladyfinger halves; brush with juice and top with mascarpone mixture. Cover lightly and refrigerate for at least 4 hours or overnight.

Whip remaining 1½ cups (375 mL) cream. Mound over trifle, leaving rim of mascarpone mixture visible. Dust rim lightly with more sifted cocoa powder. Garnish with chocolate curls and fresh raspberries.

Serves

8-10

*To substitute for mascarpone cheese, beat ½ cup (125 mL) sour cream and 2 tbsp. (30 mL) of butter into 16 oz. (500 g) of cream cheese.

Light and Heavenly Strawberry Tiramisu

When you want to indulge and behave, this is your dessert!

¾ cup	sugar	175 mL
½ cup	Egg Beaters	125 mL
2 tsp.	vanilla	10 mL
12 oz.	nonfat cream cheese	1½ x 250 g
2 tbsp.	gelatin (2 x 7 g env.)	30 mL
¼ cup	cold water	60 mL
8	egg whites	8
2 cups	light whipped nondairy topping	500 mL
20	ladyfingers (approx.)	20
3 cups	sliced strawberries and juice	750 mL
2 cups	chopped low-fat chocolate cookies	500 mL
	whole strawberries	

Method

Process sugar, Egg Beaters, vanilla and cheese until smooth and creamy. Dissolve gelatin in water and heat in medium microwave about 30 seconds. Beat into cheese mixture. Beat egg whites until stiff and fold into cheese mixture along with whipped topping.

Line a 10" (25 cm) springform pan with plastic wrap. Dip ladyfingers in strawberry juice and place on bottom of pan. Top with strawberries. Spoon half of cheese mixture over strawberries. Top with half of chopped cookies. Repeat layering, ending with chopped cookies. Cover with plastic wrap and chill overnight. Unmold tiramisu and decorate with whole strawberries.

Serves

6-8

Pumpkin Frangelico Bread Pudding with Coffee Cream

To "lighten up" simply use the lighter substitutes suggested.

9	thick slices white bread	9
3 tbsp.	butter	45 mL
14 oz.	can pumpkin	398 g
1 cup	milk	250 mL
1 cup	heavy cream or evaporated skim milk	250 mL
¼ cup	molasses	60 mL
½ cup	brown sugar	125 mL
2	large eggs	2
2 tsp.	cinnamon	10 mL
1 tsp.	ginger	5 mL
1 tsp.	allspice	5 mL
1 tbsp.	vanilla	15 mL
¼ tsp.	salt	1 mL
¼ cup	Frangelico	60 mL
½ cup	sugar	125 mL
2 tbsp.	water	30 mL
18	pecan halves	18

Coffee Cream:

1 cup	chilled whipping cream or 1 cup (250 mL) nonfat sour cream	250 mL
1 tbsp.	instant coffee powder	15 mL
2 tbsp.	brown sugar	30 mL
1 tbsp.	coffee liqueur or Frangelico	15 mL

Method Butter the slices of bread and cut into large cubes. Place ⅓ of the cubes in the bottom of a buttered 9" (23 cm) springform or bundt pan.

Whisk together the pumpkin, milk, cream, molasses, brown sugar, eggs, spices, vanilla and salt. Ladle about 2 cups (500 mL) pumpkin mixture over bread cubes in pan. Top with ⅓ more bread cubes and then ⅓ pumpkin. Shake pan and let set about 15 minutes. Top with remaining bread and pumpkin. Pour the Frangelico over top. Place baking pan in a larger pan of hot water. Bake at 350°F (180°C) about 45 minutes, or until set.

Caramelized Pecans: In a saucepan, combine the sugar and water and cook over medium-high heat until caramel colored. Watch closely. Remove from heat and stir in pecans. Remove pecans, 1 at a time, and place on a foil-lined, greased baking sheet to cool and harden.

Coffee Cream: Whip cream with remaining ingredients. Remove cooled pudding from pan. Cover with coffee cream; decorate with pecans. To serve pudding warm, decorate with pecans; serve cream on the side.

Serves 8-10

Strawberry Shortcake To Live For with Chantilly Cream

The ultimate favorite of the men in my life – my three boys and my dad!

Shortcakes:

2	eggs	2
¾ cup	sugar	175 mL
1 tsp.	vanilla	5 mL
	pinch of nutmeg	
1 tbsp.	grated lemon zest	15 mL
⅓ cup	flour	75 mL

Chantilly Cream:

1 cup	low-fat whipped topping, whipped	250 mL
1 cup	nonfat sour cream	250 mL
2 tbsp.	icing sugar	30 mL
1 tbsp.	fresh lemon juice	15 mL
1 tbsp.	lemon zest	15 mL

Strawberry Filling:

2 cups	fresh strawberries	500 mL
2 tbsp.	icing sugar	30 mL
	lemon zest, for garnish	

Method

Shortcakes: Lightly spray 6 muffin cups with a nonstick coating. Beat eggs and sugar until thick and creamy, about 5minutes. Beat in vanilla, nutmeg and lemon zest. Gently fold in flour. Pour into muffin cups and bake at 350°F (180°C) about 15 minutes, or until golden.

Chantilly Cream: Gently whisk all ingredients together. Chill. Toss sliced strawberries with icing sugar. Split cooled shortcakes and fill with cream. Top with more cream and mounds of strawberries. Garnish with lemon zest.

Serves 6

Cream Cheese Strudel

Very European – very wonderful.

⅓ cup	sherry	75 mL
1 cup	raisins	250 mL
2 x 8 oz.	cream cheese, at room temperature	2 x 250 g
½ cup	icing sugar	125 mL
2	eggs	2
½ tsp.	vanilla	2 mL
1 tbsp.	finely grated orange rind	15 mL
16	leaves phyllo pastry (preferably fresh)	16
1 cup	melted butter	250 mL
⅓ cup	apricot preserves	75 mL
1 tbsp.	sherry	15 mL

Method

Bring ⅓ cup (75 mL) sherry to a simmering boil. Add raisins. Simmer about 5-10 minutes. Set aside. This will "plump" the raisins. Cream the cheese, sugar, eggs, vanilla and orange rind together. Stir in raisins. Set aside.

Take 1 sheet phyllo, brush with melted butter, top with second sheet of phyllo, brush with butter. Repeat this procedure, using about 8 sheets of phyllo.

Mix the apricot preserves with the 1 tbsp. (15 mL) sherry.

Brush top phyllo sheet with ½ of the apricot preserves. Spoon ½ of the cream cheese filling along the long side of phyllo stack. Tuck in ends. Roll as for a jelly roll. Slash top. Brush with melted butter. Repeat the procedure with remaining 8 sheets of phyllo and remaining filling. Bake both strudels on an ungreased cookie sheet at 400°F (200°C) for about 30 minutes. When slightly cool, sprinkle icing sugar across top of strudels.

Serves

12

Mango and Cream Cheese Empanadas

What a great picnic or lunch treat instead of pie.

Flour Tortillas:

2 cups	flour	500 mL
1½ tsp.	baking soda	7 mL
1½ tsp.	salt	7 mL
5 tbsp.	shortening	75 mL
¾ cup	hot water	175 mL

Mango Filling:

14 oz.	can mangoes or peaches, well drained	398 mL
8 oz.	cream cheese, softened	250 g
3 tbsp.	icing sugar	45 mL

Method

Flour Tortillas: Combine flour, baking powder and salt in bowl. Cut in shortening until mixture resembles coarse meal; do not over process. Add hot water and gently mix and knead for 10-15 seconds. Cover bowl and let dough rest 15 minutes. Divide dough into 12 balls. Roll dough balls in flour, put in plastic bag and let rest for another 20 minutes. Roll each ball into a 4" (10 cm) circle and let rest.

Filling: Pat dry and slice mangoes or peaches. Beat softened cream cheese with icing sugar. Place 1 large slice of mango and 1 large scoop of cheese in each tortilla. Fold over and seal edges. Bake at 400°F (200°C) for about 10 minutes, until golden. Pat with paper towel. Sprinkle with icing sugar.

Serves 12

Variations: Mascarpone cheese may be substituted for cream cheese.

Mile-High Lime Pie

Very refreshing – very light. Serve with raspberry or strawberry coulis* (below).

Crumb Crust:

1½ cups	graham crumbs	375 mL
2 tsp.	cinnamon	10 mL
3 tbsp.	light margarine	45 mL

Lime Filling:

2 tbsp.	gelatin (2, 7 g env.)	30 mL
¼ cup	cold water	60 mL
14 oz.	can evaporated skim milk	398 mL
½ cup	sugar	125 mL
½ cup	lime juice	125 mL
1	lime, zest of	1
4 tbsp.	frozen lime concentrate	60 mL
	green food coloring (optional)	

Meringue:

4	egg whites	4
1 tsp.	cream of tartar	5 mL
⅓ cup	sugar	75 mL
3 tbsp.	water	45 mL

Method

Crust: Mix crust ingredients together and press into deep 9" (23 cm) pie plate. Bake at 365°F (185°C) about 10 minutes.

Filling: Dissolve gelatin in cold water. Stir. Heat in microwave at medium for 1 minute. Beat milk only until soft peaks form. Beat in sugar, juice, zest and concentrate. Stir in gelatin. Pour into cooled pie shell. Chill thoroughly.

Meringue: Beat egg whites and cream of tartar until stiff. Bring sugar and water to a boil, and simmer about 3-5 minutes, to soft-ball stage. Slowly add sugar syrup to egg whites, beating constantly.

Top pie with meringue and broil until golden, watch carefully to avoid burning meringue.

Serves 6-8

*Fresh Fruit Coulis: A coulis is a thick purée or sauce. Purée fresh berries or seasonal fruit such as peaches or mangos; add sugar to taste. Add a few drops of Grand Marnier or Cointreau, if you wish.

Raspberry Velvet Tart

What a valentine!

Chocolate Crust:

¾ cups	all-purpose flour	175 mL
½ cup	sugar	125 mL
6 tbsp.	cocoa	90 mL
⅛ tsp.	salt	0.5 mL
6 tbsp.	butter	90 mL
¾ tsp.	vanilla	3 mL
3 tsp.	water	45 mL

White Chocolate Raspberry Filling:

12 oz.	white chocolate, chopped	340 g
½ cup	whipping cream, heated	125 mL
¼ cup	butter	60 mL
2 cups	raspberries	500 mL

White Chocolate Leaves:

3 oz.	melted white chocolate	85 g
6	large green leaves	6

whipped cream
raspberries
grated white or dark chocolate

Method

Crust: Combine flour, sugar, cocoa and salt in processor. Add butter and process on and off until crumbly. Blend in vanilla and water. Gather dough into a ball, wrap in plastic wrap and chill. Roll out dough and fit into 9" (23 cm) tart pan. Chill 30 minutes. Bake at 350°F (180°C) for 15 minutes. Cool.

Filling: Melt white chocolate over simmering water. Mix in hot cream and butter. Remove from heat. Let cool slightly. Spoon raspberries over crust. Pour chocolate mixture over raspberries. Chill until firm.

Leaves: Paint the underside of washed and dried leaves with melted chocolate. Chill until hard. Carefully peel off leaves.

Decorate the pie with whipped cream, raspberries and grated chocolate. Place white chocolate leaves around edges.

Serves   6-8

Nectarine and Mascarpone Tartlet

If you haven't discovered mascarpone cheese – do it this way!

Pie Crust:

1 cup	all-purpose flour	250 mL
2 tsp.	sugar	10 mL
½ tsp.	grated lemon peel	2 mL
⅛ tsp.	salt	0.5 mL
7 tbsp.	chilled unsalted butter, cut into pieces	105 mL
1	egg yolk	1
2 tbsp.	cold water	30 mL

Peach Glaze:

¾ cup	peach preserves	175 mL
2 tsp.	kirsch	10 mL
1 tsp.	fresh lemon juice	5 mL

Nectarine Mascarpone Filling:

6 oz.	mascarpone cheese	170 g
¼ cup	icing (powdered) sugar	60 mL
2 tsp.	kirsch or other brandy	10 mL
1 tsp.	vanilla extract	5 mL
4	small nectarines, pitted, sliced	4
4	fresh mint sprigs (optional)	4

Method

Crust: Combine flour, sugar, lemon peel and salt in a processor. Add butter and process using on/off turns until mixture resembles coarse meal. Add yolk and water and process until large moist clumps form. Gather dough into ball; flatten into disk. Wrap in plastic and chill 30 minutes.

Roll out dough into roughly a 10" (25 cm) round. Transfer round into 10" (25 cm) flan pan with removable bottom. Gently press round into place. Trim edges. Pierce bottom of crust with fork. Freeze until dough is very firm, about 30 minutes. . Bake crust at 400°F (200°C) until golden, about 15 minutes. Cool crust completely

Glaze: Bring peach preserves, kirsch and lemon juice to a boil in a small heavy saucepan. Strain. Cool slightly.

Filling: Whisk mascarpone, icing sugar, kirsch and vanilla extract in a small bowl until smooth. Brush sides of crust with peach glaze. Spread filling evenly over crust. Arrange nectarine slices attractively over filling. Brush nectarines with peach glaze.

Refrigerate tart until filling is set, about 30 minutes. Remove tart from pan and garnish with fresh mint sprigs, if desired.

Serves

4

Grand Marnier Apricot Pumpkin Pie in Walnut Crust

The pumpkin filling is prebaked and spooned into the baked, glazed crust. What a do-ahead treat for pumpkin fanatics.

Apricot Pumpkin Filling:

½ cup	diced apricots	125 mL
	Grand Marnier to cover	
14 oz.	tin pumpkin	398 mL
½ tsp.	ground ginger	2 mL
1 tsp.	cinnamon	5 mL
½ tsp.	salt	2 mL
¾ cup	sugar	175 mL
¼ tsp.	ground nutmeg	1 mL
⅛ tsp.	ground cloves	0.5 mL
1¾ cups	half-and-half cream	425 mL
2	eggs, beaten to blend	2

Walnut Crust:

1 cup	flour	250 mL
¼ cup	finely ground walnuts	60 mL
½ tsp.	salt	2 mL
3 tbsp.	butter, well chilled and cut into small pieces	45 mL
2 tbsp.	solid vegetable shortening, well chilled (Crisco works well)	30 mL
3-4 tbsp.	ice water	45-60 mL
2 tbsp.	apricot preserves	30 mL

Topping:

1 cup	whipping cream	250 mL
1 tbsp.	sugar	15 mL
1 tbsp.	Grand Marnier	15 mL
	walnut halves and dried apricots	

Method

Filling: Soak apricots in Grand Marnier to cover, at least 4 hours or overnight before proceeding with the recipe.

Crust: Combine flour, walnuts and salt in processor, cut in butter and shortening using on/off turns. With machine running, pour 3 tbsp. (45 mL) ice water through feed tube and mix just until dough comes together. Use more water as needed. Roll out on a floured board and fit into a 9" (23 cm) pie plate. Trim and form edges. Chill. Bake in 425°F (220°C) oven about 15 minutes, or until golden brown. Cool completely. Brush bottom and sides with preserves.

Filling: Drain Grand Marnier from apricots; reserve. Combine pumpkin, ginger, cinnamon, salt, sugar, nutmeg and cloves. Stir in Grand Marnier. Blend cream with eggs; whisk into pumpkin mixture. Fold in apricots.

Grand Marnier Apricot Pumpkin Pie in Walnut Crust

Continued

Bake in a 6-cup (1.5 L) shallow casserole at 425°F (220°C) for 15 minutes. Reduce temperature to 350°F (180°C). Bake 50 minutes more, until top of custard cracks. Cool completely. Spoon custard into crust, spreading evenly.

Topping: Beat cream with sugar and Grand Marnier. Spoon over custard, covering completely. Decorate with walnuts and apricots.

Serves   6-8

Sedated Strawberries in Chocolate

¼ cup	Grand Marnier or other liqueur	60 mL
12	large strawberries, rinsed and well-dried	12
	melted white chocolate	
	melted dark chocolate	
	ground pecans (optional)	

Method   Fill a plastic syringe with liqueur. Carefully inject into strawberries. Let strawberries rest about ½ hour. Dip ends into melted white or dark chocolate, then into nuts, if using. Chill until chocolate sets.

Makes   12

Exotic Fruit Sabayon

This can be prepared ahead and broiled at the last minute.

1 cup	dry champagne	250 mL
5	large egg yolks	5
⅓ cup	sugar	75 mL
1	papaya, peeled, seeded, sliced	1
1	mango, peeled, pitted, sliced	1
3 cups	raspberries	750 mL
¾ cup	chopped peeled pineapple	175 mL

Method   Whisk first 3 ingredients in a medium metal bowl. Set bowl over saucepan of simmering water (do not allow bowl to touch water) and whisk until candy thermometer registers 160°F (71°C), about 8 minutes. Remove bowl from heat. Preheat broiler. Divide fruit among 6 large gratin dishes. Pour sabayon over. Broil until golden brown, about 1 minute. Serve immediately.

Serves   6

Brandied Orange Babas

I love to package these and give them as gifts at Christmas!
But they do have a refrigeration life of only about 1 week.

Babas:

1 tbsp.	instant yeast	15 mL
2 tbsp.	sugar	30 mL
1 tsp.	salt	5 mL
2 cups	flour	500 mL
½ cup	milk	125 mL
4 tbsp.	butter	60 mL
2	eggs	2

Brandied Orange Sauce:

2 cups	water	500 mL
2 cups	sugar	500 mL
1	lemon, thinly sliced	1
1	orange, thinly sliced	1
½ cup	orange brandy	125 mL

Topping:

½ cup	apricot preserves	125 mL
	red and green glacé cherries	
	whipped cream	

Method Combine yeast, sugar, salt and ½ cup (125 mL) flour. Heat milk and butter until warm. Add liquids to first mixture and beat 2 minutes. Gradually beat in eggs and ½ cup (125 mL) of flour. Beat 2 minutes. Stir in 1 cup (250 mL) flour. Cover and let rise until doubled. Grease large muffin tins well and spoon in the dough. Let rise again for 30 minutes. Bake at 350°F (180°C) for 20-25 minutes.

Sauce: Bring to a boil the first 4 ingredients. Simmer 10 minutes. Remove from heat and add orange brandy.

Remove baked babas and place in a baking dish. Prick all over with a toothpick. Pour sauce over and baste. Keep turning babas to absorb sauce. Melt the apricot preserves and brush over babas. Garnish with red and green cherries. Serve warm with whipped cream.

Serves 12

Pictured on page 87.

Dessert

Croquembouche, page 180

Pears Bella Helena

4	large pears	4
	lemon juice	
1½ cups	walnuts or pecans, chopped	375 mL

Ricotta Filling:

1 cup	ricotta cheese	250 mL
3 tbsp.	icing (powdered) sugar	45 mL
2 tbsp.	Frangelico	30 mL
2 tsp.	lemon zest	10 mL
½ tsp.	freshly grated nutmeg	2 mL
2 oz.	semisweet chocolate, finely chopped	55 g
2 tbsp.	chopped ginger	30 mL

Method Wash, peel and halve pears. Remove cores and brush with lemon juice.

Filling: Beat first 3 ingredients in processor until smooth. Fold in lemon zest, nutmeg, chocolate and ginger.

Fill pear cavities with ricotta filling. Dip filled pears in chopped nuts. Chill. Serve with warm Chocolate Frangelico Sauce, below.

Serves 6

Variation: **Peach Bella Helena:** Marinate peeled pitted peaches in 1 cup (250 mL) dry white wine and 2 tbsp. (30 mL) brandy. Omit chopped chocolate from filling. Proceed as above.

Chocolate Frangelico Sauce

½ cup	whipping cream	125 mL
2 tbsp.	sugar	30 mL
5 oz.	semisweet chocolate, chopped	140 g
2 tbsp.	Frangelico	30 mL

Method Combine cream and sugar and heat. Stir in chocolate until it melts and add Frangelico. Serve warm.

Peach Flambé

¼ cup	butter	60 mL
2-3	whole cloves	2-3
¼ cup	Demerara sugar	60 mL
3	whole fresh peaches, sliced (canned sliced peaches may be used)	3
¼ cup	whipping cream	60 mL
4 tbsp.	liqueur of choice (for this recipe I use kirsch)	60 mL

Method In a chafing dish or saucepan melt butter over very low heat. Sauté cloves for 2 minutes. Remove cloves. Stir in Demerara sugar, just until dissolved. Stir in sliced peaches. Sauté until thickened (sauce should be thick and dark). Slowly stir in cream. Heat liqueur and ignite. Pour flaming liqueur over peaches. If you prefer not to flame liqueur, just stir it into peach mixture.

Serve in individual dishes over French vanilla ice cream.

Serves 6

Apricot Gratin with Almonds and Kirsch

Another souvenir from France – dry apricots also work, but do remember to make it during fresh apricot season!

Step 1 – For Fresh Apricots Only (24 hours ahead):

1 cup	superfine sugar	250 mL
½ cup	honey	125 mL
1	vanilla bean	1
2½ cups	water	625 mL
2¼ lbs.	fresh apricots or 4 x 14 oz. (398 mL) canned	1.25 kg

Step 2 – If using Canned Apricots:
Topping:

¾ cup	icing (powdered) sugar	175 mL
1¼ cups	almond powder	300 mL
10 tbsp.	unsalted butter	150 mL
2	egg yolks	2
1	whole egg	1
¼ cup	slivered almonds	60 mL
3 tbsp.	apricot brandy or kirsch	45 mL

Apricot Gratin with Almonds and Kirsch

Continued

Method

Step 1: If using fresh apricots, the preparation should be begun at least 24 hours ahead. If using canned apricots eliminate the first step.

For fresh apricots, combine 1 cup (250 mL) sugar, the honey, vanilla bean and water in a large saucepan and bring to a boil. Add the whole apricots and bring back to a boil over medium-high heat. Remove from the heat. The apricots should be completely submerged in the syrup. If not, they will discolor. If necessary, invert a saucer on top of the fruit to keep it submerged. Cover the saucepan and let stand for 24 hours. During this overnight marinating, the pits will impart an almond flavor to the apricots and their syrup.

Drain the fruit, reserving the syrup, being careful not to crush the apricots. Halve the apricots. Remove and discard the pits. Place 4 or 5 apricot halves in the bottom of each of 4 small gratin dishes, arranging them to just cover the bottom of the dishes.

Step 2: If using canned apricots, begin the preparation at this point. Drain the fruit; reserve the syrup. Arrange 4 or 5 apricot halves in the bottom of each gratin dish, or enough to cover the bottom of the dishes.

Place the remaining fresh or canned apricots in a food processor with a little of the syrup and process to a thick purée. Set aside.

Topping: Combine ½ cup (125 mL) of the powdered sugar, the almond powder, butter, egg yolks and whole egg in a mixing bowl. Beat with a whisk until thoroughly blended.

Divide the batter among the 4 gratin dishes, spreading it evenly over the apricots. Sprinkle the top of the batter with slivered almonds. Sprinkle the remaining ¼ cup (60 mL) of sugar over the gratin dishes with a sugar sifter or fine sieve.

45 minutes before serving, preheat the oven to 425°F (220°C). 20 minutes later, place the gratin dishes in the oven and bake for 15-20 minutes, until lightly browned on top.

Just before serving, place the apricot purée in a small saucepan and warm over low heat. Add the apricot brandy and pour the sauce into a warmed sauceboat.

Place the gratins on dessert plates to serve. Pass the apricot topping separately.

Serves   4

Croquembouche

This Victorian dessert is a spectacular centerpiece.

Pâte à Choux Puffs:

¾ cup	unsalted butter	175 mL
1½ cups	water	375 mL
¼ tsp.	salt	1 mL
1 tsp.	sugar	5 mL
1½ cups	sifted all-purpose flour	375 mL
6	large eggs	6

Glaze:

1	egg beaten with	1
1 tsp.	water	5 mL

Mocha Crème Pâtissière:

6	egg yolks	6
½ cup	sugar	125 mL
½ cup	sifted all-purpose flour	125 mL
2 cups	milk	500 mL
3 tbsp.	unsalted butter	45 mL
2 oz.	semisweet chocolate	55 g
2 tsp.	instant espresso	10 mL
2 tsp.	hot water	10 mL
2 cups	whipping cream, whipped	500 mL

Caramel:

2 cups	sugar	500 mL
⅔ cup	water	150 mL
2 tbsp.	corn syrup	30 mL

Method Preheat oven to 425°F (220°C).

Puffs: Melt butter in water with salt and sugar. Remove from heat, add flour, return to heat and beat vigorously for 2-3 minutes. (A film should form on bottom of pan and dough should pull away from sides of pan.) Cool slightly, and add eggs, 1 at a time, beating vigorously. Using a pastry tube with a ½" (1.3 cm) opening, form 1" (2.5 cm) high mounds, ¾" (2 cm) in diameter, on parchment-lined baking sheet. Combine egg and water to make glaze. Glaze and smooth the tops. Bake for 20-25 minutes, until puffed and golden. Cool on racks.

Mocha Cremè: Beat egg yolks, gradually add sugar until mixture is thick and pale. Beat in flour. Scald milk; add slowly, reserving ½ cup (125 mL) for thinning. Return to a clean pot and stir vigorously over high heat until mixture boils and thickens. If too thick to pipe, add reserved milk. Remove from heat. Add butter 1 tbsp. (15 mL) at a time. Melt chocolate and add to mixture with espresso. To assemble, inject cream into puffs with a ¼" (6 mm) pastry tip. Top puffs with whipped cream and freeze in a single layer.

Croquembouche

Continued

Caramel: Bring sugar, water and corn syrup to a boil over high heat. Do not stir. Cover pan until steam dissolves any crystals. Uncover and boil 5 minutes, or until syrup is amber. remove from heat. Dip the bottoms of the frozen puffs, 1 by 1, into the caramel and arrange in a pyramid. To form caramel fragments pour liquid caramel onto a foil-lined baking pan. Let harden and then break into pieces. Use to decorate Croquembouche. Freeze finished Croquembouche until serving – no more than 3-4 hours.

Serves 12-20

Pictured on page 175.

Decadent Chocolate Mocha Cake

Another fat-free fantasy – as rich a chocolate cake as you could ever wish!

1½ cups	flour	375 mL
1 cup	sugar	250 mL
1 cup	cocoa	250 mL
1¼ tsp.	baking soda	6 mL
1 tsp.	baking powder	5 mL
½ tsp.	salt	2 mL
3	egg whites	3
¾ cup	strong coffee	175 mL
½ cup	nonfat milk	125 mL
⅓ cup	corn syrup	75 mL
2 tsp.	vanilla	10 mL

Chocolate Glaze:

⅓ cup	cocoa	75 mL
1 cup	icing sugar	250 mL
7½ oz.	jar baby food prunes	213 mL
2 tsp.	vanilla	10 mL

Method Sift dry ingredients into a large bowl. Add liquids. Whisk until smooth. Pour into well-greased bundt pan. Bake at 350°F (180°C) for 35-40 minutes, or until a toothpick inserted into center comes out clean. Cool.

Glaze: Whisk all ingredients until smooth. If too stiff, add small amount of hot water. If too thin, add more icing sugar. Drizzle glaze thickly across top of cake. If desired, serve with a pool of fruit purée, such as mango or raspberry.

Makes 1 bundt cake

Butter Pecan Matzo Crisps

12	matzo crisps	12
⅓ cup	butter	75 mL
⅓ cup	brown sugar	75 mL
⅓ cup	chopped pecans	75 mL
1 tsp.	vanilla	5 mL
½ cup	chocolate chips (optional)	125 mL

Method Foil a cookie sheet and spray with nonstick spray. Lay matzo crisps on cookie sheet. In a heavy pan heat butter and brown sugar until bubbly. Add chopped pecans. Bring to a rolling boil, then boil for 1-2 minutes. Remove from heat. Stir in vanilla and pour hot butter pecan mixture on matzos, spreading quickly and evenly.

Bake at 375°F (190°C) 3-6 minutes, until crisp. Sprinkle hot crisps with the chocolate chips, if using. Cool. Break into chunks. Can be frozen or kept in an air-tight container.

Cranberry Chocolate Chippers

1 cup + 2 tbsp	flour	310 mL
½ tsp.	baking soda	2 mL
2 tbsp.	finely chopped orange zest	30 mL
6 tbsp.	white sugar	90 mL
6 tbsp.	brown sugar	90 mL
½ cup	butter (8 tbsp.)	125 mL
1	egg	1
2 tsp.	vanilla	10 mL
1½ cups	fresh cranberries	375 mL
½ cup	walnuts	125 mL
1 cup	chocolate chips	250 mL
	melted dark chocolate, for garnish	

Method Mix flour and baking soda and set aside. In food processor with the metal blade, process orange zest and sugars until well mixed. Add the butter, cut in small pieces, and process until smooth and creamy. Add egg and vanilla and mix until smooth. Add cranberries, walnuts and chocolate chips and mix until blended. Drop the batter by rounded tablespoons (20 mL), 2" (5 cm) apart on a greased cookie sheet. Bake for 20 minutes at 350°F (180°C). Drizzle with dark chocolate.

Makes 12 large cookies

Low-Fat Lemon Biscotti

Wonderful dipped in strong coffee.

¼ cup	chopped hazelnuts	60 mL
2¼ cups	flour	550 mL
1½ tsp.	baking powder	7 mL
1 tsp.	ground allspice	5 mL
¼ tsp.	salt	1 mL
¾ cup	sugar	175 mL
⅓ cup	light margarine	75 mL
3	egg whites	3
2 tsp.	vanilla	10 mL
1 tsp.	lemon extract	5 mL
4 oz.	semisweet chocolate, melted	115 g
1 tbsp.	lemon zest	15 mL

Method Toast the hazelnuts and set aside. Into a large bowl sift the dry ingredients, except the sugar. In another bowl, beat sugar and margarine until light and fluffy. Beat in egg whites and flavorings. Stir in dry ingredients and toasted nuts. Shape dough into 2 logs, each about 2" (5 cm) wide and 12" (30 cm) long. Place on greased cookie sheet and bake at 325°F (160°C) about 25 minutes, or until golden. Remove from oven and cool slightly. Cut the logs in diagonal slices about 1" (2.5 cm) wide. Return to oven and bake 10 minutes longer. Cool. Drizzle small teaspoons of the melted chocolate back and forth across each biscotti. Sprinkle with lemon zest.

Makes 12

Lace Biscuits

¼ cup	sliced almonds	60 mL
4 tbsp.	liquid glucose (or equal parts sugar and water)	60 mL
¼ cup	butter	60 mL
½ cup	brown sugar	125 mL
⅔ cup	flour	150 mL
	melted dark chocolate, for garnish	

Method Finely chop almonds. Combine glucose, butter and brown sugar in saucepan and stir over low heat until sugar is dissolved and butter is melted. Bring to a boil, quickly remove from heat; stir in flour and almonds. Drop by a teaspoonful onto a greased cookie sheet, about 3" (6.5 cm) apart and bake at 350°F (180°C) 5-7 minutes. Drizzle with dark chocolate and remove cookies to wire rack right away.

Makes 10-12

Chocolate-Dipped Cappuccino Shortbread

For a gift, put these in a beautiful coffee mug and wrap in colored cellophane.

4 tsp.	instant coffee	20 mL
1 cup	butter, at room temperature	250 mL
½ cup	sugar	125 mL
½ tsp.	vanilla	2 mL
1¾ cups	all-purpose flour	425 mL
¼ cup	cornstarch	60 mL
6 oz.	semisweet chocolate, melted	180 g

Method Finely crush instant coffee in coffee grinder. In a large bowl, cream together butter and sugar. Beat in instant coffee and vanilla. Sift flour and cornstarch together; stir into butter mixture. Mold into the shape of large coffee beans, using 1 tbsp. (15 mL) of dough for each cookie. Using the back of a knife, press an indent about ⅛" (3 mm) deep, lengthwise, across the top of each cookie. Place on a greased cookie sheet.

Bake at 325°F (160°C) for 15 minutes. Place on wire racks to cool. Dip both ends of cookies in chocolate. Place on baking sheet lined with wax paper and refrigerate.

Makes about 3 dozen

Pecan Wafers

Sandwich these delicate, crisp cookies with ganache or dip in chocolate for a more elegant presentation.

1 cup	unsalted butter, room temperature	250 mL
1 cup	sugar	250 mL
2	egg whites, room temperature	2
1 lb.	pecans, toasted and finely ground	500 mL
¼ cup	all-purpose flour	60 mL
¼ tsp.	salt	1 mL

Method Using electric mixer, cream butter until light. Add sugar and beat until light and fluffy. Add whites, 1 at a time, beating until a smooth paste forms. Combine pecans, flour and salt. Using a spoon, fold into batter. Spoon rounded teaspoonfuls (10 mL) batter onto greased cookie sheets spacing 2" (5 cm) apart. Bake at 300°F (150°C) until cookies are golden brown, about 10 minutes. Cool on racks. Store in an airtight container.

Makes about 5 dozen

Beverages

Turquoise Margaritas

Blue Curaçao provides the color, and lime peel the freshness.

6	lime slices	6
	coarse salt	
6¼ oz	frozen limeade	178 mL
1 cup	water	250 mL
½	lime, quartered	½
¼ cup	tequila	60 mL
¼ cup	blue Curaçao	60 mL
4 cups	ice cubes	1 L

Method Rub lime slices around rim of each of 6 stemmed glasses. Reserve lime slice. Dip rims of glasses into salt. Combine Margarita mix and next 3 ingredients in blender. Blend until lime is finely minced. Add ice and blend until thick and smooth. Pour into glasses and garnish with lime slices.

Makes 6 servings

Pictured on page 69.

Ruby Red Margarita (Tequila and Pink Grapefruit Cocktail)

1	lime wedge	1
	coarse salt for coating rim of the glass	
1½ oz.	tequila (1 jigger)	45 mL
3 tbsp.	fresh pink grapefruit juice (preferably ruby red)	45 mL
1 oz.	orange-flavored liqueur	30 mL
½ tsp.	superfine sugar if desired	2 mL
1 cup	ice cubes	250 mL
¼	of a slice of ruby red grapefruit for garnish	¼

Method Rub the rim of a cocktail glass with the lime wedge, dip the rim of glass into salt, coating it lightly; chill the glass. In a blender, blend the tequila, the grapefruit juice, the liqueur, the sugar and ice cubes for 30 seconds. Pour the drink into the glass and garnish it with the grapefruit slice.

Makes 1 drink

Mangoritas

14 oz.	tin mango slices, drained or	398 mL
	1 cup (250 mL) mango purée	
6¼ oz.	can limeade	178 mL
1 cup	water	250 mL
½ cup	tequila (or less, or more)	125 mL
2 cups	ice cubes	500 mL

Method Blend ingredients in blender until slushy.

Serves 4

Sherry-Champagne Cocktail

A very special Saint Valentine's toast for a very special occasion!

25 oz.	bottle dry sherry	750 mL
6¼ oz.	tin frozen pink lemonade	178 mL
	concentrate	
	crushed ice	
	chilled Asti Spumante or champagne	

Method Combine sherry and lemonade concentrate in a large pitcher and mix well. Store in refrigerator at least 24 hours but preferably longer.

Fill champagne glasses with crushed ice. Fill ½ full with sherry-lemonade. Top with chilled Asti Spumante or champagne.

Serves 10

Rhubarb Sparklers

1	medium lemon sliced	1
2 tbsp.	lemon juice	30 mL
2 cups	rhubarb purée	500 mL
3 cups	lemon mineral water	750 mL
3 cups	grapefruit soda	750 mL
3 cups	white wine	750 mL
	ice	

Method Combine all ingredients. Add lots of ice. Serve.

Serves 10-20

Summer Citrus Punch

7 cups	orange juice	1.75 L
3 cups	white wine	750 mL
1½ cups	grapefruit juice	375 mL
¾ cup	fresh lime juice	175 mL
¾ cup	fresh lemon juice	175 mL
⅓ cup	sugar	75 mL
50	ice cubes	50
1	orange, sliced	1
1	lemon, sliced	1
2 cups	strawberries	500 mL
	additional ice cubes	

Method Combine first 6 ingredients in punch bowl. Stir until sugar dissolves. Add 50 ice cubes, orange slices, lemon slices and berries and stir gently to combine. Fill glasses with additional ice. Ladle punch into glasses and serve.

Makes about 13 cups

Melon Slush

16 oz.	melon (cantaloupe, honeydew), peeled and sliced	500 g
6 oz.	can frozen lemonade	178 mL
6 oz.	can frozen limeade	178 mL
48 oz.	club soda	1.36 mL
25 oz.	white wine	750 mL

Method Purée melon and frozen drinks in blender. Place in large bowl and add club soda and white wine to taste. To make ahead, refrigerate blended mixture and add soda and wine just before serving.

Serves 10

Pineapple Sangria

4 cups	white wine	1 L
2 x 48 oz.	tins pineapple juice or concentrate plus water to make 96 oz. (2.72 L)	2 x 1.36 L
	pineapples slices, kiwi slices, etc.	
4 oz.	tamarind syrup (or other)	125 mL
2 x 25 oz.	bottles club soda or mineral water	2 x 750 mL
	ice	

Method Mix all ingredients together, adding soda and ice last.

Serves 20

Cranberry Orange Sangria

40 oz.	cranberry cocktail	1.14 L
25 oz.	dry red wine	750 mL
6¼ oz.	can frozen orange juice	178 mL
	concentrate, thawed	
1	orange	1
25 oz.	soda water, chilled	750 mL
1 cup	fresh cranberries	250 mL

Method Combine cranberry cocktail, wine and orange juice in a large pitcher and stir until well mixed. Slice orange thinly and cut each slice in half. Add soda water to cranberry mixture just before serving. Pour into goblets and garnish with fresh cranberries and orange slices.

Serves 12

Homemade Spiced Mulled Wine

This adds a wonderful fragrance at Christmas time.

1 qt.	cranberry juice	1 L
1 qt.	red wine	1 L
1	spice bundle (recipe below)	1
1	orange or lemon, thinly sliced	1

Method In saucepan place juice, wine, spice bundle and orange or lemon slices. Bring to simmer and simmer for 20 minutes, allowing flavors to blend.

Makes 2 quarts (2 L)

Spice Bundle

3	cinnamon sticks, broken in ½	3
2 tsp.	whole cloves	10 mL
3-4	star-shaped anise	3-4
1-2 strips	dried citrus peel	1-2
2-3	cardamom pods	2-3

Method For each bundle tie ingredients into a 6" (15 cm) square of cheesecloth using a string.

Makes 6 bundles

Spicy Mulled Cider Mix

¾ cup	crushed cinnamon sticks	175 mL
¾ cup	chopped dried orange rind	175 mL
⅓ cup	whole allspice	75 mL
¼ cup	whole cloves	60 mL

Method In a jar, combine cinnamon, orange rind, allspice and cloves.

Makes about 2 cups (500 mL)

Spiced Mulled Cider

4 cups	apple juice (or half apple and half cranberry juice)	1 L
2 tbsp.	Spicy Mulled Cider Mix (above)	30 mL

Method In saucepan, combine apple juice and Spicy Mulled Cider Mix. Cover and bring to simmer. Gently simmer for 20 minutes; strain into mugs.

Serves 4

Berry Eggnog Punch

12 oz.	can frozen cranberry-raspberry juice cocktail concentrate, thawed	355 mL
1 qt.	dairy eggnog, chilled	1 L
12 oz.	can lemon-lime carbonated beverage, chilled	355 mL
½ cup	whipping cream, whipped	125 mL
	nutmeg	
	fresh raspberries (optional)	

Method Combine cranberry-raspberry juice cocktail and eggnog in a pitcher. Carefully add lemon-lime beverage. When serving, add a dollop of the whipped cream to each serving. Sprinkle with nutmeg. Top with a fresh raspberry, if desired.

Makes 14, 4-oz. (125 mL) servings

Pictured on page 87.

Cappuccino Eggnog

A delicious combination that is rich but not too rich.

6	eggs, beaten	6
2 cups	milk	500 mL
⅓ cup	sugar	75 mL
1 tbsp.	instant espresso powder or 4 tsp.(20 mL) instant coffee crystals	15 mL
¼ cup	light rum	60 mL
1 tsp.	vanilla	5 mL
1 cup	whipping cream	250 mL
2 tbsp.	sugar	30 mL
	freshly grated nutmeg (optional)	

Method Mix eggs, milk, the ⅓ cup (75 mL) sugar, and espresso or coffee powder in a large, heavy saucepan. Cook and stir over medium heat about 8 minutes, or until mixture coats a metal spoon. Remove from heat. Cool quickly by placing the pan in a sink or bowl of ice water and stirring for 1-2 minutes. Stir in rum and vanilla. Cover surface with plastic wrap. Chill 4-24 hours.

At serving time. beat whipping cream and the 2 tbsp. (30 mL) sugar with an electric mixer on medium speed until soft peaks form. Transfer chilled egg mixture to a punch bowl. Fold in whipped cream mixture. Serve at once. Sprinkle each serving with nutmeg, if desired.

Makes 10, 4-oz. (125 mL) servings

Caffè D'Aldina

12	egg yolks	12
1½ cups	sugar	375 mL
9 cups	freshly brewed strong coffee	2.215 L

Method Using an electric mixer, beat yolks and sugar in large bowl until pale yellow and thick. Stir in hot coffee and beat until frothy. Ladle coffee into cups. Serve immediately.

Serves 12

The Magic of Candlelight Cuisine

I have always been a romantic. I fell madly in love with Terry, my husband, when I was seventeen and decided that I wanted to feel that way forever. Luckily for me, Terry felt the same way and our life has been – literally – champagne and roses ever since. But, I could never have known at that time that my romantic nature and my passion for cooking would combine to provide for me a unique career direction.

When we married 24 years ago, we started our life together in a tiny cottage overlooking the Pacific Ocean. Terry was still attending university, an all-star football player who eventually became a professional with the B.C. Lions Football Team. It was then that we began a ritual we still follow. Every Friday evening we shared a romantic candlelight dinner.

Cooking has always been a passion with me and while every meal was lovingly prepared, there was none as special as the one I prepared each Friday night. I'd begin my preparations by moving our little round table from its usual location to a vantage position at the picture window overlooking the ocean. On the table would go a floor-length round tablecloth, with a pretty contrasting square cloth on top. The antique dishes given me by Terry's grandmother were carefully unpacked, along with my good silver, linen napkins, and candles in elegant silver holders. Finally, I'd chill the wine. When I heard Terry's car coming up the long driveway, I'd hurriedly light the candles. As he walked in the door, sore and tired from practice, his face would literally beam at the sight of our beautiful table. That huge smile made everything absolutely perfect. From that delicious moment, throughout the dinner and the long hours of conversation, a kind of magic flooded our little cottage.

That was 24 years ago, little has changed, yet much has changed. Terry and I still share our Friday candlelight dinners and our wonderful love. Often we share our Friday table with our sons, Shaun and Bryn, now grown and having inherited their Dad's love of my cooking.

The pleasure and magic of these Friday evenings have imparted in me a desire to share with others. Candlelight Cuisine is not just another cookbook. It is a way of life. It is discovering that beautiful food, presented in an ambience of love and warmth, can become one of the most powerful ingredients in creating a happy, fulfilling lifestyle.

Share the Magic Soon!

Jane Bailey

Menus

A Candlelight Christmas

Holiday Dinner Rolls (page 40) with
Cranberry butter (page 56)
Honey Orange Potato Swirls (page 86)
Golden Baked Onions (page 94)
Boned Turkey Breast with Apricot Stuffing (page 125)
Brandied Orange Babas (page 174)

Cozy Winter Bistro Night

Cream of Reuben Soup (page 66)
Sunflower Seed Bread (page 50)
Barbecued Pork Loin with Caramelized Onions (page 130)
Mango and Cream Cheese Empanadas (page 168)

Winter Fireside Picnic

Broccoli & Mushroom Salad (page 73)
Rustic Picnic Loaf with Rosemary Chicken (page 123)
Fresh Fruit Plate with Sedated Strawberries in Chocolate (page 173)

Cupid's Fantasy Valentine's Dinner

Wine-Soaked Camembert with Toasted Almonds (page 11)
Tomato & Grilled Zucchini Salad (page 73)
Pink Potatoes (page 85)
Filet Mignon with Whisky Sauce (page 133)
White Chocolate Blancmange with Brandied Fruit Purée (page 160)

Appetizers for Two

Seafood Bisque (page 65)
Mediterranean Baked Brie (page 11)
Jerk Chicken Salad in Endive Spears (page 80)
Chocolate Coconut Phyllo Triangles with French Vanilla Ice Cream (page 159)
End of Summer Herb Bread (page 48)

Friends and Appetizers Party

Grilled Vegetable Antipasto Platter (page 95)
Crostini de Polenta (page 9)
Pesto Prawn Pizzas with Artichokes (page 10)
Brie en Brioche (page 12)
Bacon-Wrapped Chutney Bananas (page 16)
White Chocolate Macadamia Nut Terrine
with Mango and Raspberry Purée (page 162)

Something Simple Tonight

Cheddar Cheese Bread (page 43)
Crab and Spinach Torte (page 142)
Caesar Salad with Tortellini and Asparagus (page 76)
Bittersweet Chocolate Mousse with Orange Brandied Mousse (page 161)

Saturday Night and A Movie

Bacon Wrapped Scallop Salad with
Pears in Pear Vinaigrette (page 79)
Fiesta Loaf (page 8)
Spinach Ravioli with Basil Cream Sauce (page 108)
Strawberry Shortcake To Live For with Chantilly Cream (page 166)

Special Soup & Salad Night

Sourdough French Bread (page 42) with
Tomato Basil Butter (page 55)
Bouillabaisse of Vegetables (page 60) with Garlic Red Pepper Rouille (page 54)
Spinach & Cashew Salad with Pear Vinaigrette (page 71)
OR Honey Walnut Chicken Salad (page 81)
Chocolate Mocha Cheesecake with Papaya Strawberry Sauce (page 148)

Lighten Up

Pesto-Stuffed Mushrooms (page 19)
Herbed Cottage Cheese Loaf (page 49)
served with balsamic vinegar and a few drops of olive oil
Caesar Salad to Live For (page 75)
Lemon Linguine with Garlic, Clams and Mussels (page 109)
Light & Lovely Café Crème Brulée (page 162)

Let's Do Italian!

Herbed Focaccia (page 34) with
Layered Cheese Dip (page 7)
Sun-Dried Caesar Wedges (page 76)
OR Sautéed Pepper & Salami Salad (page 82)
Anniversary Rotolo with Chicken & Scallops (page 111)
Pears Bella Helena with Chocolate Frangelico Sauce (page 177)

Dinner on the Riviera

Mediterranean Baked Brie (page 11)
Sun-Dried Tomato Bagels (page 39)
Succulent Seafood Risotto with Sun-Dried Tomatoes and Spinach (page 138)

Seafood Supper with Friends

Middle Eastern Bread Salad (page 74)
Pesto French Bread (page 41)
Seafood Lasagne (page 110)
Light Lemon Cheesecake (page 147)

Summer Seafood Grill

Danish Blue Herb Bread (page 7)
Potato Caesar Salad with Prosciutto (page 77)
Chilean Bass with Fruit Salsa (page 137)
Exotic Fruit Sabayon (page 173)

Summer Evening Dinner Party

End of Summer Herb Bread (page 48)
Barbecued Corn with Sun-Dried Tomato Butter (page 99)
Wild Mushroom Phyllos (page 19)
Goat Cheese Pasta Salad with Tomatoes and Basil (page 78)
Fragrant Spice-Crusted Pork with Mango Chutney Sauce (page 129)
Blackberry Bread Pudding with Chantilly Cream (page 152)

Romantic Summer Barbecue

Turquoise Margaritas (page 186)
Quesadillas with Brie, Mango & Chilies (page 14)
Grilled Vegetable Antipasto Platter (page 95)
Basil Nectarine Flatbread (page 33)
Mustard-Coated New York Steak with Horseradish Sauce (page 131)
Peach Flambé (page 178)

Feeling Friday

Spicy Stuffed Crab (page 25)
Shredded Wheat Bread (page 48)
Fruity Spinach Salad with Raspberry Poppyseed Dressing (page 68)
Breast of Chicken Medallions with
Brandied Apples & Pink Peppercorns (page 116)
Ultra-Light Ultimate Cheesecake with Fruit Purée (page 146)

Something To Celebrate

Spinach, Brie & Walnut Salad (page 68)
Sun-Dried Tomato Poppyseed Flatbread (page 36)
Grilled Tequilla Salmon (page 136)
Strawberry Shortcake To Live For with Chantilly Cream (page 166)

Sunday Family Dinner

Almond-Chive Bread (page 45)
Red Hot Potato Wedges (page 85)
Mango Carrots with Pine Nuts (page 90)
Roast Prime Rib with Red Wine Pepper Sauce
and Red Onion Marmalade (page 132)
Caramel Apple Cheesecake with Peaches (page 144)

Very Vegetarian!

Veggie Cheese Pâté (page 6)
Homemade Herbed Boboli (page 37)
Tortellini of Artichokes & Marscapone (page 105)
Apple Spinach Slaw (page 74)
Fried Sweet Cream (page 157)

Intimate Thanksgiving

Glazed Pecan Biscuits (page 31)
Chunky Almond Dressing (page 54) over Butter Lettuce
Boneless Turkey Breast in Phyllo Pastry with
Green Peppercorn Sauce (page 127)
Cranberry-Kumquat Relish (page 56)
Pumpkin Frangelico Bread Pudding with Coffee Cream (page 165)

Index

SHARE *CANDLELIGHT CUISINE* WITH A FRIEND

Order *Candlelight Cuisine* at $18.95 per book plus $4.00 (total order)
for shipping & handling.

Number of copies _____ x $18.95 = $ _____

Shipping and handling charge_____ = $ ___4.00___

Subtotal_____ = $ _____

In Canada add 7% GST_____(Subtotal x .07) = $ _____

Total enclosed _____ = $ _____

U.S. and International orders please pay in U.S. funds./ Price subject to change.

Name: _____

Street:_____

City: _____ Province/State: _____

Country: _____ Postal/Zip Code:_____

Please make cheque or money order payable to: **Brenda Johnson**
918 - 12th Street
New Westminster, British Columbia
Canada V3M 6B1

For fundraising or volume purchases, contact Brenda Johnson.
Please allow 3-4 weeks for delivery.

SHARE *CANDLELIGHT CUISINE* WITH A FRIEND

Order *Candlelight Cuisine* at $18.95 per book plus $4.00 (total order)
for shipping & handling.

Number of copies _____ x $18.95 = $ _____

Shipping and handling charge_____ = $ ___4.00___

Subtotal_____ = $ _____

In Canada add 7% GST_____(Subtotal x .07) = $ _____

Total enclosed _____ = $ _____

U.S. and International orders please pay in U.S. funds./ Price subject to change.

Name: _____

Street:_____

City: _____ Province/State: _____

Country: _____ Postal/Zip Code:_____

Please make cheque or money order payable to: **Brenda Johnson**
918 - 12th Street
New Westminster, British Columbia
Canada V3M 6B1

For fundraising or volume purchases, contact Candlelight Cuisine.
Please allow 3-4 weeks for delivery.